75
C5
D67
1988

D1270863

YOU CAN HAVE A CHURCH LIBRARY

Start, Enhance, and Expand Your Religious Learning Center – A Step-by-Step Guide for Church Leaders

Maryann J. Dotts

94451

THE GRAHAM LIBRARY
TBC - ELLENDALE. N. D. 58436

Abingdon Press

YOU CAN HAVE A CHURCH LIBRARY

Revised edition copyright © 1988 by Maryann J. Dotts
Originally published as THE CHURCH RESOURCE LIBRARY
Copyright © 1975 assigned to Maryann J. Dotts

Second Printing

All rights reserved.
No part of this work may be reproduced or transmitted in any form or
by any means, electronic or mechanical, including photocopying and
recording, or by any information storage or retrieval system, except as
may be expressly permitted by the 1976 Copyright Act or in writing
from the publisher. Requests for permission should be addressed in
writing to Abingdon Press, 201 Eighth Avenue, South, Nashville, TN
37202.

This book is printed on acid-free paper.

Library of Congress Cataloging-in-Publication Data

DOTTS, MARYANN J.
    You can have a church library / Maryann J. Dotts—rev. ed.
p.   cm. — (Called to serve series)
Rev. ed. of: The church resource library, c 1975.
Bibliography: p.
ISBN 0-687-04604-1 (pbk.: alk. paper)
    1. Libraries, Church. I. Dotts, Maryann J. Church resource
library. II. Title. III. Series.
Z675.C5D674 1988
027.6'7—dc19   88-2635
                                                                    CIP

The "Class Packet File Headings" chart on pages 47-48
is used by permission of Graded Press.

The Dewey numbers printed on pages 34-39 are
reproduced from editions 19 and 11 of the Dewey
Decimal Classification, published in 1979, by permission
of the Forest Press Division, Lake Placid Education
Foundation, owner of copyright.

Manufactured by the Parthenon Press at
Nashville, Tennessee, United States of America

CONTENTS

I. **A RESOURCE CENTER FOR LEARNING**...5

    Definition
    Church Resource Library Users

II. **DEVELOPING A RESOURCE LIBRARY**...6

    Sponsorship
    Library Committee
    Statement of Purpose
    Selection Policy
    Financing
    Location

III. **PROCEDURES**...9

    Getting a Library Started
    Register the Library
    Selecting Materials
    Ordering and Acquisitions
    Records to Keep
    Use of the Library
    Training the Staff
    Evaluation
    Promotion of the Library

IV. **PROCESSING BOOKS FOR CIRCULATION**...15

    Examine the Book
    Accession
    Ownership Stamp
    Classifying
    Call Numbers
    Card Catalog
    Making Cards
    Shelf List Card File (Optional)
    Tracings
    Book Jackets
    Book Plates
    Book Spine
    Shelving the Books
    Rules for Filing Catalog Cards
    Weeding

V. **PROCESSING MEDIA MATERIALS FOR CIRCULATION**...22

    What Are Media Materials?
    An Integrated Card Catalog
    Accession Numbers
    Making Cards
    Ownership Markings
    Specific Types: Filmstrips and filmslips, games, kits, maps, models, dioramas, globes, motion pictures, "movies," films, film loops, pamphlets, clippings, periodicals or magazines, pictures, posters, photographs, recordings, slides, transparencies

VI. SPECIAL COLLECTIONS...32

BIBLIOGRAPHY.. 32

Library Resources
Equipment and Supplies
Book Lists
Lists of Media

APPENDIX I..34

Dewey Subject Classification System for Church Resource Libraries

APPENDIX II.. 40

Subject Headings

APPENDIX III.. 47

Headings for a Picture File and Flannel Board

I. A RESOURCE CENTER FOR LEARNING

If you received an invitation to attend an open house for your church resource library, what would you expect to see when you got there? One picture that may come to your mind might be a collection of books on many subjects such as Bible reference books, theology, and devotional literature. Your mind's eye may see this in a separate room. But what else might you find on those shelves? Books for family use and Bible stories, perhaps? Books for young readers?

Your expectations are right so far. But there is more. In a church resource library there should be additional items that help support the teaching-learning activities such as maps, videos, filmstrips and slides, records and models. Many libraries include good biographies and historical novels as exciting recreational reading for all ages.

Some church resource libraries have special features such as an international doll collection, a clipping file of local church history, videotapes or slides of events in the life of the congregation, back issues of selected periodicals.

By now you can see that your visit to the church resource library would reveal not only an area with many books on shelves, but also a wide variety of materials and equipment that persons can use in teaching-learning situations or at home, both as individuals and as leaders in the congregation.

DEFINITION

What, then, is a church resource library? What is it really supposed to do? A church resource library is a collection of all the teaching-learning materials that are available for use in the life of the church fellowship. This includes both books and nonbook materials. This manual will give you basic information for selection, processing, storing, and circulating all these types of resource materials.

When you visit a classroom and see teaching materials in dusty piles on open shelves or in closets, you must ask yourself, What type of stewardship is practiced here? Teaching areas should have the materials and equipment needed, but when the leaders and students are finished with the materials they should be properly stored in a place that allows other persons to find them in good condition. Thus, at any one time, all such materials not currently being used should be stored in the church resource library where they are readily available for someone else to use them.

Where these materials are located varies. Some congregations operate several mini-libraries: one in the preschool area and one each for elementary children, youth, and adults, each located in or near those classrooms. Other congregations choose a single area to house all the materials. Each congregation needs to decide what will work best for its own situation.

Thus, good stewardship is being demonstrated when you have materials cataloged in one central place. Then potential users can come and find what is available in the card catalog and be directed to the place or places where these items are stored. This is called an integrated catalog. If you have libraries in several locations, you will need additional catalogs in those rooms, with at least title cards. Audiovisual materials and equipment, as well as books, are costly to replace, so plan wisely for their storage and use.

CHURCH RESOURCE LIBRARY USERS

To what audience are the services of a church resource library directed? Teachers and group leaders are probably the largest category of users, if they find the kind of materials they need in the library collection. You will also find children are heavy library users when there are books of a wide variety for their enjoyment.

Here are some typical examples of uses of a church resource library. An official of a local church board or committee should find the book of rules that will answer questions about church polity. A member of a senior high group will find recreation and program ideas for evening fellowship. The teacher of an older elementary class might locate slides to use in the study of an art masterpiece. A young adult planning team may look there for simulation games for their group to use. Young parents may choose storybooks for their preschool children. An adult class may be searching for a video on the life of Jesus. A task force planning a curriculum unit should find copies of study books and guides, ongoing curriculum materials, reference works, pictures, maps, and magazines. All these and many other persons in the church should find the materials they need in the church resource library.

II. DEVELOPING A RESOURCE LIBRARY

How do you know you need a resource library?

The need for a church resource library may be seen in any of the following situations:

- **You have many resources (books, pictures, filmstrips, etc.) in your congregation, but they are scattered about in many rooms, closets, and shelves.** How can a resource library gather these together?
- **You have resources that few people know about and that are not being used.** How can a resource library help promote already available materials?
- **Persons who are looking for specific resources for their teaching sessions cannot find what they are looking for.** How can an integrated catalog or filing system help busy teachers and leaders?
- **No one is giving any maintenance care to the resources and equipment.** How can this be provided through a resource library?
- **Your local public library does not have many materials on the various aspects of Christian education and the Christian faith.** How can a church resource library supplement the weak areas in the public library?
- **Few members of the congregation subscribe regularly to important church-related periodicals.** What can a church resource library do to make these current readings available to members of the congregation?

You can probably check off certain of these statements as applicable in your own situation and then add several more to the list. If one or more of these situations exists in your church, then it is time to consider starting a church resource library.

SPONSORSHIP

Every church library needs to get off to a good start as an official and intentional part of the total ministry of the local congregation. From the beginning the library should have an important place in the life of the local church fellowship.

The church resource library should be sponsored by the council or committee responsible for planning program in the local congregation. The proposal, including a plan for financing, would probably originate in the group responsible for education. It would finally be approved by the board or committee officially designated to administer the local church policies. This will ensure a solid basis on which to build a strong resource library from the beginning. The plan should include the naming of a library committee by the personnel committee of the church. This library committee will operate the library along with a designated librarian.

LIBRARY COMMITTEE

The library committee should meet regularly. It should include representation from all the groups the library hopes to serve. These meetings will provide an opportunity for each representative to alert the librarian to special activities, such as study programs and projects that will require resources. Some of the groups represented in the life of the congregation would be the children's leaders, youth workers, adult church-school groups, weekday groups (including day care and nursery school), men's and women's groups, teen ministry, and other programs in the life of the local congregation.

The library committee should be supportive of the librarian and the staff of volunteers, translating their needs for funds into ways of securing funding. In addition, the committee members will interpret and promote the library program to the whole church community. This manual is addressed to all who are concerned with the library, its policy, operation, and ministry.

STATEMENT OF PURPOSE

What is the purpose of your library? One of the earliest and most important responsibilities of the library committee and staff is to work out a statement of purpose. Will the church library try to compete with the local public library and have materials on all subjects? Or will you limit your holdings to the books and materials that help your people develop their Christian faith and fulfill their personhood as children of God? There may be no public library nearby. In that case you may want to broaden the scope of your library. What groups in your congregation do you hope to serve?

Will you include recreational reading for all ages? Do you want to minister to the community as well as to the congregation? These are the kinds of questions that must be answered in the process of developing a statement of purpose.

A written statement of purpose should specify why the library is needed, the scope of the materials offered, who can use the library, the name of the sponsoring organization, and how the funding will be made available.

A small committee may be appointed to write a purpose statement and submit it to the library committee for refinement and preliminary affirmation. Then present it for approval to the group responsible for education in the congregation. When formally approved, this statement becomes a guide for the functioning of the library. It helps in the selection of materials, in receiving budget and space assignments, in caring for materials and in encouraging the use of the collection. A copy of this policy should be posted for persons to read.

The following is a sample of one church resource library's statement of purpose:

The Church Resource Library

of _____(name)_____ Church, under

the auspices of _____(group)_____ , was

organized on _____(date)_____ for

the purpose of providing teaching-learning materials for the fellowship of _____(name)_____ Church. The library staff may accept funds through the church treasurer and gifts of materials that help to accomplish this purpose. Specific rules or guidelines for operating the library are determined by the library staff.

_____
(Librarian)

_____
(Chairperson of the
sponsoring organization)

_____
(Pastor or Chairperson
of library committee)

SELECTION POLICY

Another very important statement that must be developed in the very beginning stages is a statement of selection policy. This statement should be developed so that it helps implement the statement of purpose.

The selection policy statement should include the standard by which the library committee will judge materials as acceptable for the library collection. Write out this selection statement so that the policy covers items received as gifts as well as items purchased. A rule of thumb for gifts might be the question: Does this item meet the standards we use in selecting items for purchase? This will include the physical condition and content, as well as the way the materials fit into the overall collection. If materials are unsuitable, what would the donor prefer be done with them?

FINANCING

The sponsoring body should plan for a regular amount of money to be systematically budgeted for the expenses of maintaining the library. Funds should be handled through the financial secretary or church treasurer. In addition to this type of regular support, funds may be added to the library through a number of other means. One method includes gifts of funds given directly to the library. Another is inviting persons to pay for a book from a selected list of books needed for the library. Still another procedure is the designating of memorial money by families to remember loved ones. A fourth possibility is the giving of books to honor persons and/or events, such as a book for each church school teacher, an anniversary of the church or a long-time church leader. As a fifth alternative, classes and groups will often plan to give an amount of money each year to support the library.

In addition to regular budgeting and gifts of money, another source of income for a church resource library is gifts of appropriate books and nonbook materials. Resources obtained in this way do not have to be purchased by the library staff.

Here are a number of situations in which you can be alert to ways of acquiring materials without having to purchase them:

1. After a study course is completed invite members of the class to contribute unneeded resources to the library. These might include one copy of the study book and guide, filmstrips, packets of materials, and supplementary reading books.

2. Books the owner has finished reading and

does not want to keep can be given to the library as outright gifts. Use your selection policy statement to help evaluate such gifts.

3. At the end of each church-school curriculum quarter, invite the teachers to bring to the library one copy of curriculum resources, supplementary materials, filmstrips, records, and tapes to be accessioned into the collection.

4. When families move, persons will often donate books to the library, since they are so heavy to have moved. This is often a good way to acquire children's books.

5. Acquire the library of a retired church professional. Often retiring ministers or other church workers will donate books from their own collections in order to make them accessible to others. Here is another opportunity to use the statement of selection policy in an attempt to ensure that the books acquired in this way will be current and useful additions to the library.

6. Start a Swap Shop. This idea may not add materials to your permanent collection, but it is likely to stir up some interest in your library. By contributing one book to the Swap Shop collection, each person can take out a different book. The person can then read the book and keep it or return it to swap for another. This plan is especially good for paperbacks that you may not want to put into your permanent collection.

If funds for the library must be raised by money-making projects, use the plan of deferred spending. Raise the funds one year to underwrite the next year's expenses. This gives you an assured amount and ample time to consider how it is best to be spent for the library's present needs.

A well thought-out plan for soliciting and receiving gifts to the library should be worked out by the library committee. See "Promotion of the Library" for further ideas.

Funds for furnishings and equipment should be handled separately from the budget for purchase of library materials. In a new library the largest proportion of the initial outlay in the first years will be spent buying furniture and equipment. A library is sometimes furnished as a memorial to one or more persons who have been involved in the life of the church. When this is the case the purchase of furnishings and equipment is cared for financially; nevertheless the library staff and committee should be involved in deciding what should be purchased.

LOCATION

The location of the library may change as the collection of materials grows. At the beginning the material may be housed on some open shelving in a classroom or along a centrally located corridor in the church building. Wherever it is located, make this area as attractive as possible with special lighting, posters, and displays of materials.

If your library is located in a separate room, plan carefully to obtain the type of furniture needed to store the kinds of materials in your collection. Standard movable and adjustable furniture is recommended. Such items as adjustable shelving, card catalog, magazine racks, and reading tables and chairs will be included in most libraries. Furniture may include a file drawer for filmstrips and scripts, picture file, several comfortable chairs, an area rug, and some children's chairs. A walk-in closet is ideal for storage of media materials and equipment.

The key to the physical setting and equipment is to have what you need most for the materials you now have in your library collection. One additional goal should be to make the library an enjoyable place, so use your imagination to make this area inviting to all.

It is also helpful to store in the library area the materials used in staff work sessions. You will need a desk, a typewriter, the resource books or other materials actually being processed, the work cards, and other materials such as check-out cards, pockets, and glue. If a separate workroom is available you can arrange the space into "task areas" so that materials can progress from one step to the next along a row of tables or shelves.

In the church resource library you will find nonbook or media resources as well as books. It will be important to have on hand the kinds of equipment needed to use these various teaching-learning tools. List the kinds of materials you have and then check to see if there is adequate equipment (such as VCR, record, and cassette players, filmstrip and slide projectors) to make use of the media. You may want to use a sign-up sheet so that the equipment can be scheduled for use by leaders several weeks ahead. The equipment should be given a number, i.e., filmstrip projector #4, and signed out and in like other materials. Routine maintenance should be given to the equipment; ineffective machines will damage both the media and the reputation of your library.

III. PROCEDURES

GETTING A LIBRARY STARTED

How does a church get a new church resource library under way?

Let us assume that the preliminary steps have already been taken. That is, the need for a resource library has been felt, and an organization in the congregation has said it will sponsor the library. The pastor and/or staff have given their cooperation. A librarian and a library committee have been named for one year by the personnel committee. Plans are under way for each organization to send a representative to the library committee. The writing of statement of purpose and a selection policy is under way. A decision has been made about the appropriate place for the library. The librarian has invited persons to work as volunteers on the library staff. All these preliminary steps have been taken before anyone has touched a book or audiovisual! Now what are some things that need to be done in getting the library ready to use?

1. If possible, plan to attend a library training workshop in your area or find a librarian in another church, school, or public library who is willing to answer your questions. Write to your denominational office for information about when and where these will be held. This contact may also put you in touch with persons in your own area who will be able to help you get your library started.

The University of Utah offers a correspondence course in librarianship based on this book. For more information and cost write to University of Utah: Correspondence Study, Division of Continuing Education, 1152 Annex Building, Salt Lake City, Utah 84112.

2. Your beginning collection is whatever is available when you have gathered into one place the many materials that are scattered around the church building. You may be amazed at the size of the collection you bring together. Encourage library committee members to do this for the groups they represent. One librarian suggests weeding this collection down by at least 50 percent to materials that are current and that will be an asset to the library collection. You may begin an "old book collection" with some of the items

brought together in this way, while using the remainder of the books in an old book sale.

3. Once you have your beginning collection gathered together you will have to organize and prepare it for use. Here is a brief summary of steps to use in organizing and preparing these materials for use:

a. Separate the materials into types (all books together, all filmstrips) and then into broad subject areas like general reference works, philosophy and psychology, religion, arts, history and geography.

b. Decide on each item to determine its appropriateness for your library.

c. Make a work slip on a 3 by 5 index card for each item. The work slip serves as a model for the typist, so include all the data you will later need on the catalog card.

225
JON

Jones, Clifford M.
  New Testament Illustrations
Cambridge at the University Press
1966 (The Cambridge Bible Commentary
on The New English Bible Series)

Companion to Understanding the
New Testament
  1. Bible, N.T. — Study Guide

A work slip

d. Assign an accession number to each book, with each one receiving the next consecutive number (see ways to identify nonbook accession numbers in the section called "Processing Media Materials for Circulation").

e. Assign a call number, which includes a classification number (subject) and letters (author name).

f. Specify the subject heading that will help to identify this book in the card catalog.

g. Have cards typed for each book, including at least four card catalog cards (author, title, one or more subject cards, and shelf), book card and pocket, and typed label if spine labels are used.

h. Complete the process by attaching book card and pocket, book plate, spine label, and ownership stamp. File the card catalog cards. Then the material is ready for circulation.

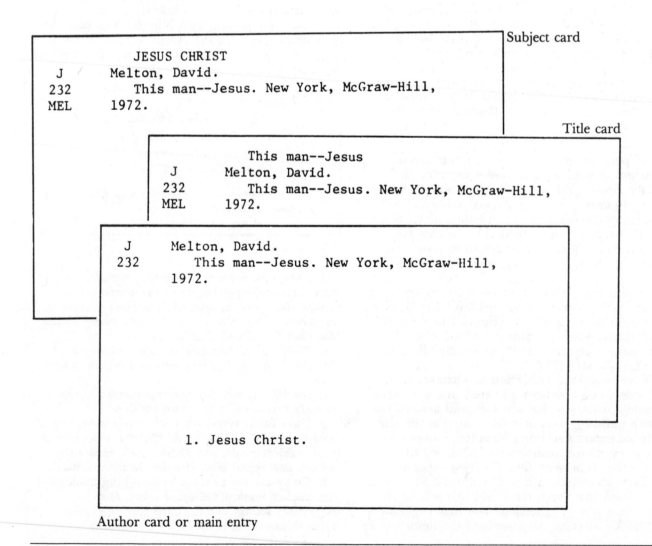

	Date	August 19, 1975							
	Accession Number	AUTHOR	TITLE	PUBLISHER	YEAR	SOURCE	COST		REMARKS
	201	Barclay, William	The Ten Commandments for Today	Harper/Row	1974	Baker	5	95	
	202	Rahner, Karl, Ed.,	Encyclopedia of Theology	Seabury	1975	Cokesbury	27	50	Memorial/ Grace Allen
28	203	Melton, David	The man-Jesus	McGraw-Hill	1972	Gift from Mrs.			CC. Reed
9/5	204	New English Bible with Apocrypha		Oxford	1970	City Books	4	95	
	05								
	06								

A page in an accession ledger

Subject card

```
          JESUS CHRIST
  J      Melton, David.
 232        This man--Jesus. New York, McGraw-Hill,
 MEL     1972.
```

Title card

```
             This man--Jesus
     J      Melton, David.
    232        This man--Jesus. New York, McGraw-Hill,
    MEL     1972.
```

```
  J      Melton, David.
 232        This man--Jesus. New York, McGraw-Hill,
         1972.




         1. Jesus Christ.
```

Author card or main entry

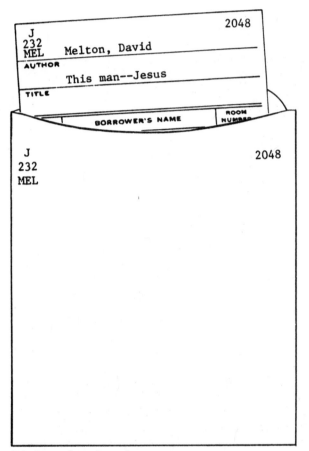

Book card and pocket

J
232
MEL

Spine label

A detailed explanation of all the steps used in preparing library materials for circulation will be found in the sections on processing.

As you work with the items in each broad category you will be aware of (1) areas in which the library does not have up-to-date resources and (2) areas in which there are no holdings at all. Keep a running list, or put these areas on cards to serve as a consideration file when information is needed to make decisions about choosing new items to order in the future.

REGISTER THE LIBRARY

After the church resource library is sponsored and a librarian is named, register the library with a bookstore or dealer that will provide the kinds of materials you need. Ask if there is a discount on books and/or other materials.

SELECTING MATERIALS

Once the librarian has organized the materials that are on hand, decisions can be made concerning additional materials. Here are some ways to determine what additional items should be added to the church's collection:

- **List the coming emphases in the life of the congregation.**
- **List the needs of special study groups through information given to the library committee.**
- **List the teaching emphases coming up in church school classes.**
- **Examine your shelf list or consideration file for any gaps in the collection.**

Book Plates

- **List the subject areas in which requests are made that you cannot fill.**

From these listings create a priority list or file that includes only those items the library committee can realistically consider adding in the near future. Include the times of the year when the materials will be needed. Keep the priority file on cards with as much ordering information as possible (including title, author, publisher, date, cost, and ISBN number given on most items) so you will get the exact item you wish. Arrange this file as to preference or date of need. Since most budgets will cover only a portion of these items, add additional titles to the list of suggested gift books. Check the card catalog to be certain that you do not already have a copy of a particular title before ordering.

There are many helps to aid the librarian in the selection of suitable materials. You will want to become familiar with many of these listed in the bibliography.

ORDERING AND ACQUISITIONS

When you have the ordering information on a book or nonprint resource, try to order it as quickly as possible so that it will be available when persons need to use it. Choose a supplier that can get materials for you from any publisher. Do not hesitate to ask questions about securing materials, and use your library discount on books purchased for the library. Keep a carbon copy of your order blanks so that you can check off the items as they are received. All bills should be sent to the church treasurer (or whoever pays the bills for the library) as soon as you have decided that the materials are appropriate for your collection. If materials are to be returned for any reason, do so immediately with an appropriate cover letter giving the details on why you are returning the items. Request the library book rate when figuring the postage.

RECORDS TO KEEP

Certain records are necessary in every library. These will include the order blanks, a record of accession numbers, the budget and expenditures.

On the accession ledger you have in one place a complete history of each item, including accession number, author, title, and price.

This accession record can be used for getting a dollar value for insurance purposes and for taking regular inventory. Keep the accession record in a fireproof place.

Keep a record of the number of items that have been checked out. This can be done by categories, such as children, adults, media.

USE OF THE LIBRARY

Have as few rules as possible and make the rules help rather than hinder the user of your library. The library is for the persons who need to use materials and grow through their use. It is not for the purpose of preserving a collection. Persons should be able to sign out books and materials and stamp them for the date due (two weeks or one month). These sign-out cards can be left on the desk and can be filed by a library staff person at a later time.

Arrange for a place for the returned resources to be deposited. Draw a line through the sign-out card so that it is easily seen that the resource was returned. Most church libraries do not use a system of fines.

Set up a policy for the follow-up of overdue materials. Send a postcard after the first month and follow later with a phone call. Encourage persons to let the library staff members know if materials are needed longer or if they cannot be found at this time.

TRAINING THE STAFF

The library staff are volunteer workers who want to serve their church in a meaningful ministry. This idea should be the basis of all that is done in the library. The routine task of preparing materials for use takes on new meaning when library staff members see these activities as helping persons in their Christian growth and understanding.

The library staff may develop good working relationships and minister to one another as persons and really have fun doing their jobs. The librarian sets the tone for this group. The staff will be involved in an ongoing training program as they work through the various tasks in preparing materials and helping persons find the materials they need.

One rule of thumb in training workers is to train at least two or three persons to do each task needed in preparing materials. This should provide someone for each time you meet, as well as allow for changes on the staff.

When should the library staff meet? You will need to decide what works best and how often you need to meet. If you are beginning a library there is much to do. Weekly meetings may be needed at the beginning. Pace your group as your need indicates. A regular meeting time works best so persons can plan to have the time available. Use whatever plan works best for getting the job done.

Some of the tasks that need to be done:
- **Have person on hand when the library is open (example: Sunday mornings) to answer requests for information, reference questions, file sign-out cards, receive returned books, place sign-out cards in them and reshelve, check out and check in audiovisual materials and equipment.**
- **Prepare materials for circulation; a regular meeting day.**
- **Change the displays and bulletin boards.**
- **Write the publicity for the church newsletter.**
- **Host groups (such as church school classes) who visit the library to learn what is available and how items may be checked out.**

- **Prepare a budget and keep a record of spending for the library.**
- **Decide on what materials are needed and order them.**
- **Review books and materials for groups.**

Write your own list of duties and make a schedule of the times persons are needed in the library. Then volunteers can sign up for the dates when they will be on duty.

EVALUATION

At the end of the year evaluate the work of the library committee and the library staff. What are the most effective ways that the library has served persons? What areas do you feel need improvement? How can this happen? Read the purpose and selection policy statements again and see how you have measured up after this year's work. Have you fulfilled the purpose? What areas need improvement? Are there some changes that could be made for more efficient ministry in your library? You may want to write these ideas down and look at them periodically until next year, when you evaluate again what has been done.

PROMOTION OF THE LIBRARY

Promotion or public relations for the library involves keeping the congregation aware of the many resources that are available in the library. This is one kind of promotion and is done through personal contact with groups and their leaders, through displays, written notes, and answering requests that come to the library. The best promotion is always a person whom you have helped.

A second phase of promoting involves raising of funds and/or gifts for the further development of the library. Funding for the library may involve making a budget and submitting it to the local church budget committee or sponsoring organization. Raising of funds may be through gifts such as memorials and remembrance gifts given by individuals or class groups. Sometimes it is necessary to sponsor some money-making activity with the proceeds going to the library budget.

Some examples of the first type of promotion—keeping people aware of what is available—are given here as thought starters. You will find many more ways to use the resources you have at hand to promote your library to the people in your congregation.

1. Print lists of subjects and titles on various reading levels in the church newsletter. Include also lists of media available for a study emphasis or for a season of the year.

2. Make a suggestion box and post your responses with a copy of the suggestion.

3. Print bookmarks with titles and authors of books for seasons or special interests (example: books in your library for Easter reading). Include them in the Sunday morning worship bulletin.

4. Create a special shelf for the books listed on the bookmark for easy access for a month after the bookmarks are given out.

5. Make colorful displays of books, seasonal items, travel posters, clippings about books; change these displays regularly.

6. Make up small traveling suitcases or cloth bags of six to eight books for families to borrow and take on trips.

7. Hold an open house for the library and invite persons to come and see what is available. A good time may be after the morning services or between church school and the worship service.

8. Sponsor a poster or bookmark contest on using the library for children and one for youth. Award a book of the winner's choice in each age division. Use the posters for publicity for the library.

9. Include the church resource library on a tour of the church building for new members.

10. Honor parents of preschool children with a coffee and show books that are appropriate to that age level. Encourage early reading aloud to children to help with reading readiness as well as to provide a creative family activity.

11. Arrange a "new materials shelf" for the latest additions.

12. Arrange a children's story hour during school vacations, day care hours.

13. Advertise that persons are available to give book reviews, or to read to persons who are unable to read (older persons, blind or convalescent persons of all ages).

14. Invite classes to visit the library to learn what is available and how to check out materials. Ask groups what they would like to see added to the library's present collection. This gives good input for further selection of materials.

15. Hold a book party. Have persons dress up as characters in a book that they have read and enjoyed. Give prizes for the most original, silliest, most elaborate, and cleverest use of materials. Plan for each person to identify his character and introduce the book to the group.

16. Sponsor a book review group, reading club, or discussion group for children or adults.

17. To get persons to sponsor gift books use a

listing of the "Ten Most Wanted Books for Our Library."

18. **Provide lists of good books for children to help adults with selection of gift books.** This may be through a book fair in which you order on consignment a number of books and sell them with the profits going to the library budget.

19. **Involve members of the library committee in keeping the groups they represent aware of the progress made in the library.**

20. **Celebrate with special reminders about such times as Children's Book Week and Church Library Week.**

21. **Write short news notes for the weekly bulletin or church newspaper.** Be positive and brief. You may want to create a longer publicity sheet by using a half-page insert in the bulletin once a month.

In the second phase of promotion—raising of funds for the library—the following ideas are merely examples:

1. **Fund-raising activities may be carried on to underwrite some of the library expenses.** There are all kinds of sales: bake sales, old book sales, new books on consignment from your book supplier, doughnuts and coffee after church or church school, desserts, a booth at a flea market for sale of old books and duplicates of teaching pictures, as well as other items given to the library for resale.

2. **Sponsor a money-making event and sell tickets in advance: a drama, a movie, a puppet show, or some other type of entertainment; a book review, fashion show and salad luncheon.**

Promotion is really a reflection of the library committee's pride and enthusiasm for the library. Let yours overflow and infect your whole congregation.

Clockwise from upper left: bookcase, magazine rack, card file, picture filing cabinet, filmstrip storage cabinet

IV. PROCESSING BOOKS FOR CIRCULATION

The goal of every librarian is to get the materials out on the shelves as soon as possible, for there they will be available for use. This is a good goal, but by the same token hasty processing of materials often causes more problems than you wish to encounter. Take the time to work out your system of processing and follow it for all materials added to the library. The section that follows details each of these steps.

EXAMINE THE BOOK

Open the book with the spine and front and back covers on the table. Press hinges until the front and back covers lie flat on the table, while holding the pages upright in one hand. With the other hand press a few pages at the back and then a few pages at the front until the middle of the book is reached. Opening the book carefully will prolong the life of the backing. Paperbacks should be opened carefully.

Check the book for the numbering of the pages. Occasionally a book has duplicate signatures (a signature is a group of pages bound as a unit), or a signature may be put in the book upside down. Are there any pages that are uncut at the edges? If so, put a sharp knife between the pages and slit them apart. If the book is in poor condition, return it to the supplier for a replacement.

On old books, look for pages missing or places that need to be repaired.

ACCESSION

Assign an accession or inventory number to each book. Number consecutively as you add each new item. Enter the number at the following places in each book:
—on the page following the title or on the title page
—on book pocket and book card (upper right-hand corner)
Keep a record of the number given to each book in an accession ledger. Put number on shelf list card, if you use this file.

OWNERSHIP STAMP

A rubber stamp with the name of the library and/or the name of the church and the mailing address should be purchased for use in the library. Stamp or hand-letter the name of the library on the following places:
—**inside front cover (or use book plates) or inside back cover**
—**back of the title page or at the bottom of the title page**
—**book pocket and sign-out card**

CLASSIFYING

Classification numbers are chosen to indicate the subject of a book. By giving all the books on one subject the same number you will find them together in one place on the shelf.

Here are some clues to help you assign classification numbers. Decide what is the main subject or topic in the book. Study the book title and the chapter titles in the table of contents to get an idea of what the book is about. Read the preface statement for the author's purpose and point of view. If the book covers more than one subject, choose the more general category and assign the classification number according to that area. Many books being published now have all the information you need for classification and cataloging on the back of the title page or at some other place in the book. This is called "CIP" (Cataloging in Publication) and contains helpful information. See the illustration to identify the various pieces of information.

It will be necessary to decide on some system of classification for new libraries. There are several, and some churches have developed their own systems. The Dewey Decimal Classification System is a widely known system and is recommended for the church resource library. In the Dewey system all areas of knowledge are divided into ten basic classes or subject areas. Look at the ten classes listed below:

000–099	General works (bibliographies and encyclopedias)
100–199	Philosophy and psychology (child psychology, ethics)
200–299	Religion (the Bible, Christian non–Christian religions)
300–399	Social science (social issues, economics, government, education)

THE GRAHAM LIBRARY
TBC - ELLENDALE, N. D. 58436

94451

400–499 Languages (English and foreign)
500–599 Science (mathematics, biology, life sciences, nature study)
600–699 Useful arts (medicine, engineering, agriculture, home economics)
700–799 Fine arts (painting, architecture, sculpture, music, theater, sports, recreation)
800–899 Literature (of all countries)
900–999 History and geography (of all countries)

Each of these ten classes is then broken down into divisions and assigned numbers as needed. Let us look at the 200 class as an example:

200–209 Religion
210–219 Natural religion (through observation, speculation, and reasoning)
220–229 Bible
230–239 Christian doctrinal theology
240–249 Christian moral and devotional theology
250–259 Local Christian church and religious orders
260–269 Christian social and ecclesiastical theology (institutional)
270–279 Church history
280–289 Denominational sects of Christian church
290–299 Non–Christian religions and comparative religion

Each of these ten divisions can be expanded by dividing still further. For example, the section on the Bible (220–229) is given below:

220 Bible
221 Old Testament
222 Historical books of the Old Testament
223 Poetic books of the Old Testament
224 Prophetic books of the Old Testament
225 New Testament
226 Gospels and Acts
227 Epistles
228 Revelation
229 Apocrypha

Each of these ten subdivisions can be divided still further by the use of decimals. Look at the subdivision on the Bible (220):

220.1 Origins and authenticity
(220.2 not used)
220.3 Encyclopedias and topical dictionaries
220.4 Original texts, early versions and translations, class concordances, dictionaries, complete texts, lower criticism, comprehensive works on texts and versions

220.5 Modern versions (English versions from 1582 to present)
220.6 Interpretation and criticism (exegesis, general introductions to Bible, symbolism, harmonies, mythological, allegorical interpretations, mythology in the Bible)
220.7 Commentaries (arranged in textual order)
220.8 Special subjects treated in the Bible
220.9 Geography, history, chronology, persons of Bible lands in Bible times (include Bible stories retold). Persons should be placed with the part of the Bible in which he/she is chiefly associated, i.e., Abraham 222

It is most likely that the majority of your books in a church resource library will be in the 200 class, and this section has been reprinted in *200 Religion Class, Dewey Decimal Classification* (Broadman Press, 1980, based on the 19th unabridged edition).

A simplified table of classification numbers for church libraries is included in Appendix I of this book. Additional help in classification is available in the book *Abridged Dewey Decimal Classification and Relative Index* (see "Bibliography").

CALL NUMBERS

A call number is a visible code symbol that distinguishes one book from another. In part, the call number results from the classification process, since the first line of the call number will be the classification number mentioned in the previous section.

The second line uses the author's last name to give some help in arranging books on the shelf. The first three letters of the author's last name form this second line.

Let's use an example. An author by the name of J. C. Custer has written a book on the Christian education of children, and you are giving it a call number. As a result of classifying the book, you will have a classification number of 268.432, which becomes the first line of the call number. The second line will be "CUS" because of the author's last name.

When an author has written several books that would have the same classification number, a "work letter" (in lower case) may be added to identify the order of those books on the shelf. Use the first letter of the title, omitting articles (a, an, the). Example:

J. B. Phillips,

God Our Contemporary	PHIg
Plain Christianity	PHIp
When God Was Man	PHIw
Your God Is Too Small	PHIy

Call numbers are the clues that tell you where to find a book on the shelf. Place a call number in the following places:

1. On the spine of the book
2. On the back of the title page
3. On the book pocket and sign-out card

There are some special cases that need to be mentioned in connection with call numbers.

Adult fiction books do not use call numbers at all, for they are arranged alphabetically by the author's last name.

For children's fiction or stories use a "JF" as the first line of the call number, with the first three letters of the author's last name as the second line. These are shelved by the author's last name.

Example: JF
CAR

Informational books or nonfiction books for children use a "J" on the first line, a classification number by subject on the second line, and the first three letters of the author's last name on the third line. Arrange these by numerical sequence.

Example: J
220.4
SMI

When more than one book has the same classification number arrange those books by author's last name.

Biographical books use a "B" on the top line and, on the second line, the letters of the last name of the person about whom the biography is written rather than the author's name. This allows all the books about one person to be together on a shelf.

Example: B   (for a biography
LUT   on Luther)

Reference books use an "R" on the top line above the classification number. These may be shelved together in one place by number or on the shelf with other books of the same subject and in numerical order.

Example: R
220.2
CRU

Books for preschool children are identified with an "E" on the first line and the first three letters of the author's last name (or the full name) on the second line.

Example: E
BAT

CARD CATALOG

The card catalog is an alphabetical index to all the materials in the library. There must be at least one card (title card) in the catalog for each item in the library, and normally there should be at least three cards for each item. These include: (1) a main entry card, usually the author card; many media pieces do not have an author, (2) a title card, and (3) one or more subject cards. All subject headings are printed in capital letters.

See Appendix II for subject headings and for ways to create additional subject headings for your library.

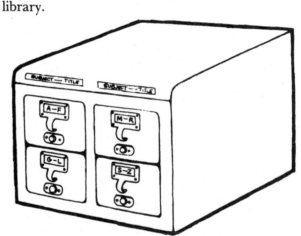

Card catalog

If a person knows the author's name, he can find the author card, get the call number, and locate the book on the shelf. If a user knows only the title of the item, it is possible to look for the title card, get the call number, and look for it on the shelf. If someone wants a book or books on a certain subject, such as prayer, sacraments, ethics, or nature study, he/she can find what the library has on these subjects if subject cards have been made.

Thus, three cards are suggested: an author card, a title card, and one or more subject cards. If an item has no author, the title card becomes the main entry card. All cards are filed alphabetically in an integrated catalog.

In addition to the basic cards, many libraries use such optional cards as "See Cards" and "See Also Cards."

It is sometimes necessary to add additional cards in order to help the user of the catalog. A "See Card" gives the user the subject area in which materials will be found. For example, if all the materials on "Youth" (in the church) are located in the subject called "Christian Education of Youth" it would be helpful to direct the user to the proper subject by means of a See Card. The See Card is filed alphabetically under the subject heading *not used,* and it directs the user to the heading that *is used* in this catalog.

```
              YOUTH MINISTRY

                   see

         CHURCH WORK WITH YOUTH
```

"see card"

```
              SACRAMENTS

                see also

         BAPTISM
         LORD'S SUPPER
         MARRIAGE
```

A "see also card"

Another optional card is the "See Also Card." You may want to let the user know that related materials may be found in other subject headings in addition to the heading now being investigated. The See Also Card does this by listing those other subject headings; it is filed before other cards of the same wording so that persons will know immediately what other subjects they may look under.

MAKING CARDS

On the work slip put all the information you need to type the cards. Make a set of spacings for the typist. Allow room for the full cataloging information at the left margin, which is the nine spaces across. Drop down two lines before beginning the author's name. This will allow

enough space to put the subject heading or a series title.

Being consistent will give your card catalog a neat appearance. Be certain to indicate to the typist the number of cards needed for each item.

```
225     Barclay, William.
BAR         The letter to the Hebrews. Philadelphia,
        Westminster Press, 1967.  (The Daily Study
        Bible Series)




            1. Bible. N.T. Hebrews-Study and Teaching
```

A main entry (author) card, showing tracing

You are now able to generate catalog cards with a computer program such as Librarian's Helper. The software uses the traditional AACR2 standards for creating catalog cards, labels for spine, book pocket, and circulation card. With one initial entry of the information about a piece of media, the cards are produced. These help the cataloger and the typist, because several functions are built into the program. See "Bibliography" for more details.

SHELF LIST CARD FILE (Optional)

The shelf list card file is an optional file that is not part of the card catalog. This file is suggested for the use of the librarian and staff. The cards are filed by call numbers and stored with the staff work materials. The work slip (see "Getting a Library Started" in "Procedures" above) may be used as a shelf list card. The shelf list card file allows you to:

- inventory the shelves to find lost, misshelved books (that is, to "read" the shelves)
- prepare bibliographies of books and resources in one area (such as a list of resources relating to the Christmas story)
- check for consistency in the assignment of classification numbers
- tell at a glance the areas that have few titles (which aids in selection of new items)

TRACINGS

Tracings are necessary when you use subject cards in your card catalog. When only title and author cards are used, there is no question about which cards to remove from the catalog when a title is no longer in your collection, such as a lost or out-of-date item. But when you do use subject cards for books and other resources, you will have to keep a record of the subjects used for a particular item. This record is the tracing, which lists headings where cards are filed for a particular item. The tracings are typed near the bottom on the main entry (or author) card.

BOOK JACKETS

Book jackets are your best promotion of a book. Keep the jacket on the book and immediately cover the book and jacket with clear plastic covers. Let the carefully designed covering of the book help "promote" it, for books that are more eye-appealing have greater circulation.

BOOK PLATES

Book plates may be secured from most book stores for use in gift books or memorial books. Separate book plates may be printed with the library name for use in all books. Glue these on the inside of the front cover.

BOOK SPINE

Call numbers should be displayed on the spine of each book in the library, or—in the case of books with narrow spines—in the upper left-hand corner of the front cover. There are several ways to place the number on the book: **(1) typed on a pressure-sensitive label and covered with translucent tape, (2) written with India ink and pen, (3) written with an electric stylus and its accompanying tape, (4) heated affixed labels with the small platen on the book spines and media boxes, or (5) added plastic covers to protect the labels.**

(1) Pressure sensitive label and translucent tape

(2) India ink and straight pen

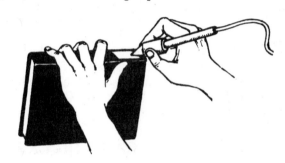

(3) Electric stylus and tape

SHELVING THE BOOKS

Arrange the books on a cart or table in numerical order according to call numbers. All books in one class will then be arranged alphabetically. This will aid you in taking them to the shelf area.

Begin arranging materials on the top shelf and move down to the bottom row of shelves, going from left to right. Begin with the smallest number and move to the larger numbers. An example of how books would appear on the shelf follows:

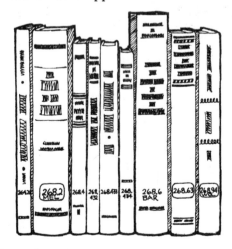

Call numbers

Note in the illustration that the decimals are followed closely. The whole number is first, followed by the first decimal, then the second or third place decimal.

When you have several books with the same number, use the last name of the author (or the first three letters of the name as shown on the second line of the call number) to arrange the books in order alphabetically.

When the last names are the same, use the first initial to decide which book will come first. Example:

Richards, Jim; Richards, Robin; Richards, William; Richards, Wilson

When there are several books by the same author arrange them by title in alphabetical order. See illustration of J. B. Phillips, page 17.

For ways to shelve children's books, biography, fiction, and reference books, see the "Call Numbers" section above.

RULES FOR FILING CATALOG CARDS

After the catalog cards are typed and checked for accuracy, add them to the card catalog. A good practice is to have one person file the cards and another person check them for accuracy. Arrange all cards alphabetically *by the first line, word by word,* alphabetizing letter by letter within the word. Each word in the entry is considered, including articles (a, an, the), prepositions, and conjunctions. However, initial articles a, an, and the are disregarded. Disregard all punctuation marks.

For example:

1. New, J. Martin (author)
2. New, John Henry (author)
3. NEW LONDON
4. NEWSCOPE
5. A NEWSPAPER CLIPPING FILE
6. NEWSPAPERS
7. New York, New York
8. The New York Times

Consider initials, single or in combination, as one-letter words. Place them before longer words with the same first letter. Arrange acronyms as words unless written in all capitals with a space or period between the letters, in which case they should be filed as initials. For example:

UNESCO (filed as an acronym)
U.N.E.S.C.O. (filed as initials)

Arrange abbreviations as if spelled out in full. For example:

St. = Saint

Arrange names beginning with the prefixes M' and Mc as if written Mac.

Arrange numerals as if spelled out as words.

In an integrated card catalog that has more than one item with an identical title, file the book card first, then the subject card, filmstrip, model, picture, video, if all the titles or first lines are identical. For example:

Dead Sea Scrolls (book)
   DEAD SEA SCROLLS (all caps for a subject heading)
   The Dead Sea Scrolls (filmstrip)
   Dead Sea Scrolls (model)
   Dead Sea Scrolls (picture)
   Dead Sea Scrolls (video)
   Dead Sea Scrolls Translation (book)

See the following list for examples of filing order:

A B C book
African diary
A.L.A. book list (as initials)
Ambassador for Christ
BIBLE. See also
   BIBLE—NEW TESTAMENT
   and BIBLE—OLD TESTAMENT
The Bible and its story
Bible. English. Authorized
Bible. English. Authorized. Selections. 1941
   BIBLE. ENGLISH—HISTORY
   Bible. English. Revised. 1923
   Bible. English. Revised Standard. 1956
   The Bible in art
Bible in literature
Bible. N.T. Acts. English. Authorized. 1959
Bible. N.T. Acts. English. Barclay. 1957
BIBLE. N.T. COMMENTARIES
Bible. N.T. English. American Revised. 1959
Bible. N.T. Epistles. English. Phillips. 1957
Bible. N.T. Epistles of John. English.
Barclay. 1960
   The Bible of the world
Bible. O.T.
Bible. O.T. Psalms
Bible. O.T. Psalms 23
Book, William Frederick
BOOKBINDING
BOOKBINDING—HISTORY
McHaile, Kathryn
Machard, Alfred
McLaren, J. T.
St. Paul, Minnesota
Save the earth! an ecology handbook for kids
70 nature projects

WEEDING

Books and materials may need to be replaced if they become outdated or receive hard use. It is hard to know if an old book is valuable, but an experienced librarian or book dealer can help you. Old books on church history, local history, or policy manuals and yearbooks should be kept for future value. Write to your denomination's headquarters or historical society to inquire about the value of such a book. Describe it in detail, including the year it was published and its condition.

Plan to work at weeding one group of books at a time. Use the shelf list if one is kept, and remove the card catalog cards of any titles that are no longer useful for your library. Remove the book from the shelf. Note on the accession record what has happened to the book. If it is lost or removed, draw a line through the writing and add the removal date in the margin. Keep a total of how many books are removed each year. Subtract this from the accession number to get the number of books in your collection.

V. PROCESSING MEDIA MATERIALS FOR CIRCULATION

WHAT ARE MEDIA MATERIALS?

Our definition of media materials includes everything that is not a book: magazines, tapes, filmstrips, models, and all other media. The words *audiovisuals* or *media* are sometimes used to describe some of these materials.

Media materials are like books in many ways, and there are many similarities in the tasks involved in processing them for use. Nonbook materials need to be carefully selected and of high technical quality. Otherwise they are not worthy of a place in your church resource library collection. Each piece needs to be based on accurate information and suitable for the age level for which it was intended. These materials must be carefully stored and classified for circulation.

AN INTEGRATED CARD CATALOG

It is recommended that all the materials in the library, including books, tapes, filmstrips, slides, and other media, be cataloged in one place. This is the purpose of the integrated card catalog. For example, when a person is searching for materials on the Dead Sea Scrolls for older elementary students, what might he find on that subject in an integrated card catalog? The following is a sample list:

Cave of Riches by Alan Honour "J"
The Dead Sea Scriptures in English Translation by Theodor H. Caster
Dead Sea Scroll Jar (model)
The Dead Sea Scrolls (slides)
The Dead Sea Scrolls and Our Scriptures (filmstrip)
DEAD SEA SCROLLS (see picture file under BIBLE, HISTORY OF)
Discoverers of the Dead Sea Scrolls (filmstrip)
Secrets from the Caves: A Layman's Guide to the Dead Sea Scrolls
The Story of the Dead Sea Scrolls by Uriel Rappaport

Media items will be marked with an age-level indication on the card so that persons can find materials appropriate for older elementary children. The leader can make some quick judgments by the information listed on the cards, looking further at items that have possible usefulness for this age level. This could include some of the adult books on the list that might have good picture sections or be useful for advanced readers. Even this list does not exhaust the library resources on the Dead Sea Scrolls, because there are books of a more general nature such as the Bible dictionaries and the commentaries that have articles and pictures on the Scrolls as well. The librarian can help persons find these additional resources. The subject card for each of these books (DEAD SEA SCROLLS) will bring the book title into this alphabetical listing regardless of title. Example:

DEAD SEA SCROLLS
Honour, Alan. Cave of Riches . . .

ACCESSION NUMBERS

Accession each type of nonbook material with a different symbol and number; this designation replaces the usual call number. All filmstrips would be placed in one accession listing, all records in another, all games in still another. An example would be FS-25, which is the twenty-fifth filmstrip in the collection. Instead of an abbreviation, the complete designation of the materials may be used in this symbol, such as Filmstrip-25, Video-25. In such a library you will find all the filmstrips together in one storage area and at least a title card and subject card in the integrated card catalog.

Many media items with more than one type of visual or teaching material are packaged in one kit or media pack. These items should be kept together in the original box, identified as a "kit," given an accession number, and stored in the original box with all the pieces. Each piece in the kit should be given an accession number, for example, Kit #34. Indicate the wide variety of subjects and number of pieces of the media through the cards and subject headings you select for it. If a series of items is stored in a holder, for instance four or more cassette tapes, indicate each tape on a title card if each tape is on a different subject.

MAKING CARDS

The card catalog serves as the listing of all the items held in the library. This includes both book and nonbook materials, however and whenever they are stored. When you are making up the catalog cards for nonbook materials include enough information on the card for users to know whether they want to preview the item to see if it is useful for their needs. Complete information on the cards saves a great deal of wear and tear on the media, and it also saves the time of the user. For instance, think of the time used and wear on the record if each potential user had to listen to it. A brief summary of the contents will tell users what is on the record and will help them narrow the choice to one or two records. Persons will still eventually listen to the record to see if the accompaniment is suitable for their group.

Examples of title and subject card are given below with each form of nonbook materials. The subject card enables persons looking for items on a specific subject to find the materials that are available in the library. If the author is unknown, you will not have an author card; this is often true with media materials. In this case the item is cataloged by its title. If you do know the author, you may want to make an author card. Put on the card all the descriptive information about the item: size of the film or tape, length in frames or minutes, and the age level for which it was designed. Another helpful section is the summary of the contents. If a reference to a major section of the Bible or specific biblical material is known, include this information. A media kit on prayers might cover several prayers, including the Lord's Prayer. Indicate these in the summary.

OWNERSHIP MARKINGS

Each type of media presents a real challenge to place some form of an ownership mark on the acetate, game board and pieces, pictures. See the following illustration for some examples. Use a permanent marker pen or scratch acetate with a sharp edge, add a stamp to the game pieces. Puzzles often cannot be marked unless a system of colored lines are put on the back.

SPECIFIC TYPES

- *Filmstrips and Filmslips*
  Symbols: **FS for filmstrip or filmslip (a short filmslip)**
  SFS for sound filmstrips having a recorded sound track

Care and Storage: Filmstrips are rolled in plastic or metal cans, and shorter filmslips are usually stored flat in long envelopes. Each usually has a script either on film or on an accompanying printed script (which sometimes includes also a leader's guide); some have a flat record or tape cassette for the sound track. Many filmstrips are included in kits and should be given a kit accession number.

There are two basic approaches to the storage of filmstrips and filmslips. One way is to store together all the components of each item. If this is done it is wise to use the boxes in which the items were originally packaged. This allows the filmstrip can, the script, and the record or tape (if there is one) to be kept together for easy access. Boxes should be stored standing up so that all records are standing on their edges, rather than lying flat. This is preferred. Storage in the original box is preferred. On the inside of the box flap, list all the items included so that an inventory can be made in the classroom as well as at the check-in desk.

```
SFS    Shalom (Sound Filmstrip) Family Films, 1974.
24         80 frames.  color.  35mm.  record.  13 min.
       manual.

           Age Level: Junior High--Adult.
           SUMMARY: The biblical theme of "Shalom"
       integral to the unfolding of God's revelation
       in the scriptures, culminating in Jesus Christ.
       Key concepts: peace, justice, mercy, wholeness,
       hope, love, and spiritual power.

           1. Bible. 2. Justice. 3. Hope. 4. Love.
```

Title Card

```
           BIBLE
SFS    Shalom (Sound Filmstrip) Family Films, 1974.
24         80 frames.  color.  35mm.  record.  13 min.
       manual.

           Age Level: Junior High--Adult.
           SUMMARY: The biblical theme of "Shalom"
       integral to the unfolding of God's revelation
       in the scriptures, culminating in Jesus Christ.
       Key concepts: peace, justice, mercy, wholeness,
       hope, love, and spiritual power.
```

Subject Card

Another approach is to store all filmstrips together, all scripts together, all records or cassettes together. In this case a special filmstrip storage drawer is used, with all filmstrips numbered sequentially as they arrive. Corresponding scripts and guides are stored in another place and given the same number as the filmstrip. The same is done with records and/or tapes. A special cabinet is usually used to allow records to be stored standing on their edges.

Records and filmstrips should be stored away from the heat. Temperatures of about 70 degrees and humidity of about 50 percent are recommended.

Processing: Each component of the filmstrip must be stamped with the library's ownership stamp and receive the same identifying symbol and accession number: the can, the script and guide, the record or tape, the carton (if used for storage) or file folder, and the sign-out card (if one is made for each item). Use a permanent pen or scratch the acetate end of the filmstrip leader with a sharp point to put on the accession number and a shortened version of the library name or initials.

Put a list of all the contents inside the box lid so the user can check off each item when the box or bag is returned. After the box is checked in and all the pieces accounted for, you may want to put a small piece of tape across the box opening before putting it back on the shelf.

A record of the accession number for each filmstrip needs to be kept in an accession ledger separate from the one used for books. Make a book pocket and sign-out card for each filmstrip or use blank cards that are filled out by the user each time a filmstrip is borrowed.

Catalog cards will include at least the title and one or more subject cards. When making the catalog cards try to tell as much as possible about the filmstrip. Abbreviations can be used that will

tell persons the basic information they need. Give an indication in a note of the age level if it is known and a summary of the story line or topics covered. This helps persons selecting materials.

- *Games*
  ### Symbol: G or Games
  Care and Storage: Games should be stored in the producer's cartons (or boxes or cloth bags) that keep all the pieces together. A checklist of the contents helps persons make sure they have all the pieces. This list can be typed and glued to the inside top or side of the box. Sometimes the boxes need to be reinforced on the edges with cloth tape.

  Processing: Assign an accession number and apply it to the box and manual and any other pieces that you feel are important to identify. Also identify each piece with the library ownership stamp.

  Make title and subject cards as in other nonbook materials. Be sure to give sufficient information about the game (including purpose, time required to play, number of players needed, age level) so that persons can get some idea from the subject or title card if they want to consider using it.

- *Kits*
  ### Symbol: Kit
  A kit is a collection of two or more objects or media that relate to a particular subject. These are sometimes samples, replicas, or models of the real item. They may also include several different media pieces that could be used independently,

```
G    Blacks and whites (Game)  Communications,
6       Research, Machines, Inc., 1970.
        Set of cards and play money.

        Age Level: Senior High--Adult.
        SUMMARY: Vicarious view of life in a ghetto
     to understand the politics and frustrations of
     poverty.

        1. Poverty. 2. Simulations.
```

Title card

```
       POVERTY
G    Blacks and whites (Game)  Communications,
6       Research, Machines, Inc., 1970.
        Set of cards and play money.

        Age Level: Senior High--Adult.
        SUMMARY: Vicarious view of life in a ghetto
     to understand the politics and frustrations of
     poverty.
```

Subject card

```
Kit   Black pilgrimage in America (Kit)  Graded
5        Press, 1970.
         8 posters.  1 study book.  1 leader's guide.
      1 dramatic reading sheet.

         Age Level: 6th Grade--Adult.
         SUMMARY: A broad view of history and con-
      tributions of the Negro to society.
         Study book: The Negro pilgrimage by C. Eric
      Lincoln.
         Dramatic reading: "Letters to a black boy."

         1. Negro history.
```

Title card

```
        NEGRO HISTORY
Kit   Black pilgrimage in America (Kit)  Graded
5        Press,' 1970.
         8 posters.  1 study book.  1 leader's guide.
      1 dramatic reading sheet.

         Age Level: 6th Grade--Adult.
         SUMMARY: A broad view of history and con-
      tributions of the Negro to society.
         Study book: The Negro pilgrimage by C. Eric
      Lincoln.
         Dramatic reading: "Letters to a black boy."
```

Subject card

like a chart, a filmstrip, puppets, a cassette tape, and some printed work sheets.

Care and Storage: Store these items in the producer's carton if possible. List all the items included and glue this list on the outside of the box.

Processing: In making catalog cards include the title of the kit, author (if known), producer, name, date, number of items of each type in the kit, information about any leader's helps or manual, and the page numbers. Be sure to indicate suggested age level for the kit. Additional subject cards can be made for individual items that may be used separately. Identify each of these cards with a note that this item is part of a kit and give the full title of the kit. Use the same accession number on each item in the kit and on additional subject cards, and be sure each piece is clearly identified with the library name.

● *Maps*
  Symbol: M or Map
  Care and Storage: Maps may be reinforced on the back with masking tape at the fold lines and on the back top edge where they are taped or tacked for hanging. Maps may be stored rolled in

```
M    Palestine in Jesus' day (Map)  Graded Press,
1       1961.
        1 sheet.  17 by 24 inches.

     Age Level: 6th Grade--Adult.
     SUMMARY: Political divisions and places
     familiar to Jesus' life and ministry.

        1. Jesus Christ--Teaching.
```

Title card

```
           JESUS CHRIST--TEACHING
M    Palestine in Jesus' day (Map)  Graded Press,
1       1961.
        1 sheet.  17 by 24 inches.

     Age Level: 6th Grade--Adult.
     SUMMARY: Political divisions and places
     familiar to Jesus' life and ministry.
```

Subject card

mailing tubes on a shelf or folded and stored in a picture file or file folder under such subject headings as MAPS—OLD TESTAMENT, MAPS—NEW TESTAMENT.

Processing: When making up catalog cards on a map give as much identifying information as possible so that the users can tell whether they want to see if the map will help them. Identify the

area pictured and the period of time, if the map is marked for a certain historical period. Use the symbol M (or the letters "Map" and an identifying accession number on the map and on the covering) in identifying the number of the map; this number should also be placed on the covering in which it is stored. Each map should also have the library's ownership stamp on it.

● *Models, Dioramas, and Globes*
  Symbol: Mod or Model
  Care and Storage: Store in a box and label with the name and accession number. Large models that will not fit in a box may be covered with clear plastic to protect them from dust. This allows persons to see what is inside without unwrapping each time. Items can be stored on shelves or in a closet.

Processing: Make the appropriate subject cards for each item and describe it. Mark the accession number on the bottom of each item and find a way to identify it with the library's name.

```
Mod   Dead Sea scroll jar (Model)  Holy Land Crafts
3        Co., 1974.
         4 pieces.  earthenware jar.  lid.  paper
      scroll reproduction.  illustrated leaflet.

         SUMMARY: Leaflet tells story of origin,
      discovery and contents of scrolls.

         1. Model of Dead Sea scrolls.
```

Title card

```
            MODEL OF DEAD SEA SCROLLS
Mod   Dead Sea scroll jar (Model)  Holy Land Crafts
3        Co., 1974.
         4 pieces.  earthenware jar.  lid.  paper
      scroll reproduction.  illustrated leaflet.

         SUMMARY: Leaflet tells story of origin,
      discovery and contents of scrolls.
```

Subject card

● *Motion Pictures,*
  "Movies," Films, Film Loops
  Symbol: MP or Motion Picture
  Care and Storage: Films should be kept in dust-proof containers. They should be stored away from the heat in 70 degree temperature. Handle film by the edges. After repeated use the film should be cleaned and inspected for damage. All repairs should be made with the proper materials.

```
MP    Teaching and learning: grades 1 and 2 (Motion
4          Picture)  ACI Films for Geneva Press, the
           United Presbyterian Church in the U.S.A.,
           1971.
           17 min.  color.  16mm.  guide.
           Age Level: Teachers and Parents.
           SUMMARY: The meaning of the open classroom
      as applied to first and second grade classes in
      church schools.  The teacher's role is that of
      a guide, to draw out the children and involve
      them in the learning process.

           1. Teacher training. 2. Church work with
      children.
```

Title card

```
MP      TEACHER TRAINING
4     Teaching and learning: grades 1 and 2 (Motion
           Picture)  ACI Films for Geneva Press, the
           United Presbyterian Church in the U.S.A.,
           1971.
           17 min.  color.  16mm.  guide.

           Age Level: Teachers and Parents
           SUMMARY: The meaning of the open classroom
      as applied to first and second grade classes in
      church schools.  The teacher's role is that of
      a guide, to draw out the children and involve
      them in the learning process.
```

Subject card

Processing: A motion picture requires a title card and at least one subject card. In making title and subject cards the following information is needed: accession number, title, producer, date, running time (in minutes), indication of color or black and white, size of film (in millimeters), age level of audience, and a summary of content.

The storage container for each film should be marked with the library's name and film name.

- *Pamphlets and Clippings*
Symbol: VF or Vertical File
Care and Storage: A group of pamphlets and clippings on a particular subject should be kept in a vertical file. Several pamphlets on the same subject may be collected in a vertical storage box and shelved with other materials on that subject.

Processing: Make a title, author, and subject card as for other materials. Or make one subject card for each file folder heading in the vertical file. For example: FIRST NORTH STREET CHURCH—CHURCH HISTORY. Pamphlets may be accessioned and classified in the same way as books if they are to be shelved.

- *Periodicals or Magazines*
**Symbol: Per or Periodical (on the cards; no
notation on the magazines themselves)**
Care and Storage: Current magazines and curriculum materials should be kept on a display

```
VF    Downtown church celebrates 100th anniversary
           (Newspaper Clipping)  June 12, 1976.
           Filed in vertical file under First North
           Street Church--Church History.

           SUMMARY: Describes the celebration planned
      at First North Street Church.

           1. First North Street Church--Church History.
```

Title card (Pamphlets and Clippings)

```
         FIRST NORTH STREET CHURCH--CHURCH HISTORY
VF

           see vertical file.
```

Subject card (Pamphlets and Clippings)

```
Per    Christianity today.

           Back issues are kept for three years.
```

Title card (Periodicals and Magazines)

```
         CHRISTIAN EDUCATION
Per    Church teachers.
           v. 1-    1973-
           Published five times a year in February,
      April, June, September, and November.

      Journal of the Association of Church Teachers.
```

Subject card (Periodicals and Magazines)

shelf and later filed in chronological order by title on flat storage shelves or placed in magazine storage boxes.

Processing: A title card is needed, and it may include information on how long back issues are kept. Subject headings may be given to magazines with a special emphasis and should be indicated on the title cards. Be sure to label magazines and curriculum resources with the library name.

- ● *Pictures, Posters, Photographs*
  Symbol: PF or Picture File (on catalog cards only; no symbol on the pictures themselves)

Care and Storage: Pictures should be stored by subject. A full listing of subject headings for pictures is found in Appendix III. Arrange pictures in a large carton or in a file with vertical holders. Picture files are available from church and library suppliers. Also available are the folders and printed tabs for this complete picture/resource filing system.

```
PF      The rich young ruler (Picture) by Jacques
        Barosin.
        1 art print.  color.  11 by 12 1/2 inches.

        Age Level: 1st Grade--Adult.
        Scripture setting: Matthew 19:21, 22.

        1. Jesus Christ--Parables and Stories.
```

Title card

```
        JESUS CHRIST--PARABLES AND STORIES
PF
            see picture file.
```

Subject card

Processing: Write on each picture the name of the subject heading in which it is filed. This subject heading should be written in the top left-hand corner of the front of the picture, if it is not already printed there. This heading makes refiling easier. Each picture also should be identified with the library ownership stamp. Mounted and framed pictures may be given accession numbers for circulation. For example, Mounted Pic. #25. These need to be stored upright in a bin so the glass will not break. Make subject headings for these pictures.

It is not necessary to make individual card-catalog cards for each picture, but it is very helpful to make subject-heading cards for each of the subject headings in the picture file.

```
Rec  Joseph and the amazing technicolor dreamcoat
36       (Record)  Scepter Records, Inc.
         1 disc (12 min.)  33 1/3 rpm.  stereo.  libretto
included.

         Music by Andrew Lloyd Webber and lyrics by
Tim Rice.
         Age Level: 3rd Grade--Adult.
         SUMMARY: Cantata with full orchestra and pop
choir, telling story of Joseph and his coat of
many colors (Genesis 37-45).

         1. Joseph.
```

Title card (record)

```
        JOSEPH
Rec  Joseph and the amazing technicolor dreamcoat
36       (Record)  Scepter Records, Inc.
         1 disc (12 min.)  33 1/3 rpm.  stereo.  libretto
included.

         Music by Andrew Lloyd Webber and lyrics by
Tim Rice.
         Age Level: 3rd Grade--Adult.
         SUMMARY: Cantata with full orchestra and pop
choir, telling story of Joseph and his coat of
many colors (Genesis 37-45).
```

Subject card (record)

```
Cas     His son (Cassette)  Harper and Row, 1973.
30          1 tape cassette.  60 min.

            From the book by Samuel Walkov, read by
Vincent Price.
            Age Level: Junior High--Adult.
            SUMMARY: The story of the life and times
of Jesus.

            1. Jesus Christ.
```

Title card (cassette)

```
Cas     Walkov, Samuel.
30          His son (Cassette)  Harper and Row, 1973.
            1 tape cassette.  60 min.

            Read by Vincent Price from the book.
            Age Level: Junior High--Adult.
            SUMMARY: The story of the life and times
of Jesus.
```

Author card (cassette)

```
                JESUS CHRIST
Cas     His son (Cassette)  Harper and Row, 1973.
30          1 tape cassette.  60 min.

        From the book by Samuel Walkov, read by
        Vincent Price.
        Age Level: Junior High--Adult.
        SUMMARY: The story of the life and times
        of Jesus.
```

Subject card (cassette)

```
VTR     Neighbor to neighbor: ethics of concern
40          (Videotape)  January 29, 1975.
            1 tape.  15 min.  b&w.  1 inch.

        Age Level: Senior High--Adult.
        SUMMARY: Dr. John Abbot deals with the
        biblical theme of concern for others.

            1. Bible--Ethics of Concern.
```

Title card (videotape)

```
             BIBLE--ETHICS OF CONCERN
VTR     Neighbor to neighbor: ethics of concern
40          (Videotape)  January 29, 1975.
            1 tape.  15 min.  b&w.  1 inch.

        Age Level: Senior High--Adult.
        SUMMARY: Dr. John Abbot deals with the
        biblical theme of concern for others.
```

Subject card (videotape)

● *Recordings*

This category can cover all types of recordings, and a system of identifying symbols can be used or the words may be written out in full.

Symbols: Rec or Record
Cas or Cassette Tape
RRT or Reel-to-Reel Tape
VCR or Video Tape
CD or Compact Disc

Care and Storage: Recordings should be placed inside some protective covering or box to keep them free from dust as much as possible. Flat disc recordings should be placed in dust jackets in a record album cover and stored standing on edge. They should be cleaned occasionally with anti-static cloths or distilled water and lint-free cloth. Tapes

and cassettes should be kept in their boxes. Store these materials in 70 degree temperature away from direct heat. Each of these tapes may be stored in drawer-type cabinets. Cassette tapes will fit into the three by five file drawers. Drawers are made for videos as well. Label the end that will be visible, along the length of the box, in the drawer with pressure sensitive labels.

Processing: It is important that the type of tape or recording be identified in sufficient detail on the catalog card to indicate the exact type of player the user will need. Mark the accession number and ownership stamp on all parts of the recording, including album covers, boxes, or other storage parts. Accession and file the recordings in numerical order by type. For example:

Video 35, Video 36
CD-21, CD-22, CD-23

If more than one subject is on a tape or recording, give a listing of the contents on the title card and

```
S1      The Dead Sea scrolls (Slides)  Wolfe Worldwide
35          Films, 1963.
            40 slides.  color.  2 by 2.  script.

        Age Level: Senior High--Adult (selected groups).
        SUMMARY: Detailed story of events that led to
        placing the scrolls in caves and their eventual
        discovery.  Maps and background information.

            1. Bible--Dead Sea Scrolls.
```

Title card (Slides)

```
             BIBLE--DEAD SEA SCROLLS
S1      The Dead Sea scrolls (Slides)  Wolfe Worldwide
35          Films, 1963.
            40 slides.  color.  2 by 2.  script.

        Age Level: Senior High--Adult (selected groups).
        SUMMARY: Detailed story of events that led to
        placing the scrolls in caves and their eventual
        discovery.  Maps and background information.
```

Subject card (Slides)

make more than one subject card. Do not put a label on the recording or sound sheets; it will get the record off balance. An identifying number can be scratched on the inside label areas of the record.

● *Slides*

This category includes 2 by 2-inch slides and View-Master slides.

Symbol: Sl or Slide V-M or View-Master Slide

Care and Storage: Slides must be protected from the light and from fingerprints. They should be kept in a slide file, boxes, or envelopes.

Processing: Slides should have a title card and subject card (if the subject is different from the title). Sets of slides are accessioned as one item, and the individual slides may be listed in the contents on the card. Give each slide in the set the same accession number, and if there is an order to the slides use an additional Arabic number to indicate the order. For example:

Sl-35:1, Sl-35:2, Sl-35:3, Sl-35:4

● *Transparencies*

A transparency is an acetate sheet that contains information prepared for projection on a screen, using an overhead projector.

Symbol: Trans or Transparency

Care and Storage: All transparencies should be stored in manila folders or envelopes in a file or box away from dampness, heat, and dust.

Processing: When making title and subject cards include the title or topic covered, the producer, and date (if known). Indicate also the number of transparencies, the number of overlays, and their size. Place a clean piece of paper between all transparencies, especially those made on a copy machine. The clear paper will allow you to read what is on the transparency.

```
Trans  Bible map transparencies (Transparencies)
24        Broadman Films, 1969.
          10 sheets.  10 overlays.  color.  10 by 12 in.

       Age Level: Junior High--Adult.
          SUMMARY: Bible lands from period of patriarchs,
       Assyrian, Persian and Greek Empires, exodus and
       conquest, twelve tribes, Judah and Israel; Jesus'
       Galilean, Judean and Perean ministries, journeys
       of Paul, Holy Land today, map of Jerusalem.

          1. Jesus' ministry. 2. Paul--Journeys. 3. Old
       Testament--History.
```

Title card (Transparency)

```
           OLD TESTAMENT--HISTORY
Trans  Bible map transparencies (Transparencies)
24        Broadman Films, 1969.
          10 sheets.  10 overlays.  color.  10 by 12 in.

       Age Level: Junior High--Adult.
          SUMMARY: Bible lands from period of patriarchs,
       Assyrian, Persian and Greek Empires, exodus and
       conquest, twelve tribes, Judah and Israel; Jesus'
       Galilean, Judean and Perean ministries, journeys
       of Paul, Holy Land today, map of Jerusalem.
```

Subject card (Transparency)

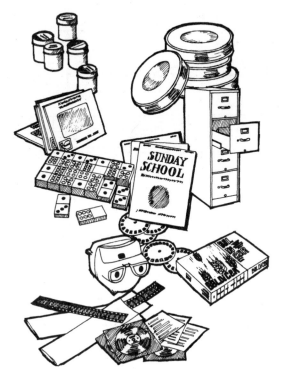

Clockwise from upper left: filmstrips in cans; metal storage containers for motion pictures; vertical file; games; filmslips with records and reading scripts; View-Master; magazines; slides

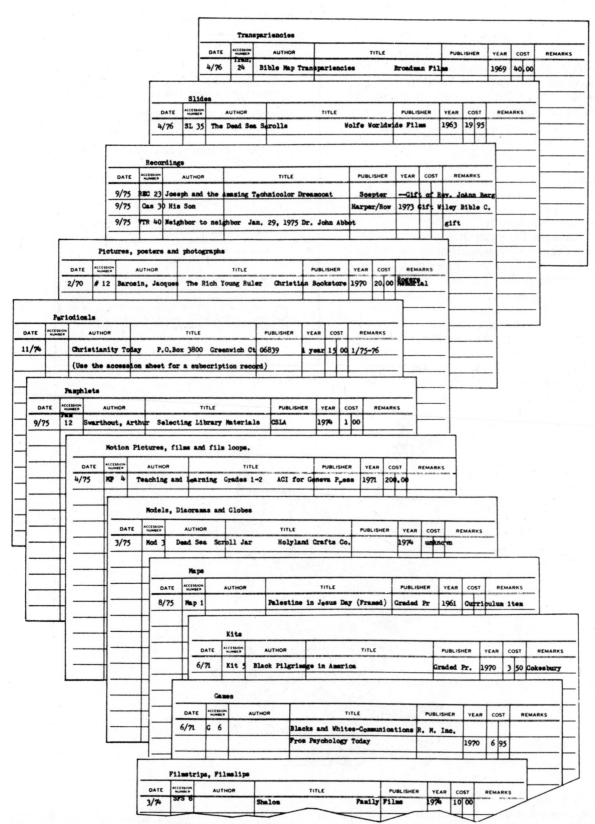

Transpariencies

DATE	ACCESSION NUMBER	AUTHOR	TITLE	PUBLISHER	YEAR	COST	REMARKS
4/76	Tran. 24	Bible Map Transpariencies		Broadman Films	1969	40,00	

Slides

DATE	ACCESSION NUMBER	AUTHOR	TITLE	PUBLISHER	YEAR	COST	REMARKS
4/76	SL 35	The Dead Sea Scrolls		Wolfe Worldwide Films	1963	19 95	

Recordings

DATE	ACCESSION NUMBER	AUTHOR	TITLE	PUBLISHER	YEAR	COST	REMARKS
9/75	REC 23	Joseph and the Amazing Technicolor Dreamcoat		Scepter			—Gift of Rev. JoAnn Berg
9/75	Cas 30	His Son		Harper/Row	1973		gift Wiley Bible C.
9/75	TTR 40	Neighbor to neighbor Jan. 29, 1975 Dr. John Abbot					gift

Pictures, posters and photographs

DATE	ACCESSION NUMBER	AUTHOR	TITLE	PUBLISHER	YEAR	COST	REMARKS
2/70	# 12	Barosin, Jacques	The Rich Young Ruler	Christian Bookstore	1970	20,00	Rogers Memorial

Periodicals

DATE	ACCESSION NUMBER	AUTHOR	TITLE	PUBLISHER	YEAR	COST	REMARKS
11/74		Christianity Today	P.O.Box 3800 Greenwich Ct 06839		1 year	15 00	1/75-76
		(Use the accession sheet for a subscription record)					

Pamphlets

DATE	ACCESSION NUMBER	AUTHOR	TITLE	PUBLISHER	YEAR	COST	REMARKS
9/75	Pam 12	Swarthout, Arthur	Selecting Library Materials	CSLA	1974	1 00	

Motion Pictures, films and film loops.

DATE	ACCESSION NUMBER	AUTHOR	TITLE	PUBLISHER	YEAR	COST	REMARKS
4/75	MP 4	Teaching and Learning Grades 1-2		ACI for Geneva Press	1971	200,00	

Models, Diaoramas and Globes

DATE	ACCESSION NUMBER	AUTHOR	TITLE	PUBLISHER	YEAR	COST	REMARKS
3/75	Mod 3	Dead Sea Scroll Jar		Holyland Crafts Co.	1974	unknown	

Maps

DATE	ACCESSION NUMBER	AUTHOR	TITLE	PUBLISHER	YEAR	COST	REMARKS
8/75	Map 1		Palestine in Jesus Day (Framed)	Graded Pr	1961		Curriculum item

Kits

DATE	ACCESSION NUMBER	AUTHOR	TITLE	PUBLISHER	YEAR	COST	REMARKS
6/71	Kit 5	Black Pilgrimage in America		Graded Pr.	1970	3 50	Cokesbury

Games

DATE	ACCESSION NUMBER	AUTHOR	TITLE	PUBLISHER	YEAR	COST	REMARKS
6/71	G 6		Blacks and Whites—Communications	R. M. Inc.			
			From Psychology Today		1970	6 95	

Filmstrips, Filmslips

DATE	ACCESSION NUMBER	AUTHOR	TITLE	PUBLISHER	YEAR	COST	REMARKS
3/74	SFS 6		Shalom	Family Films	1974	10 00	

Pages from an accession ledger showing each type of media material listed on a different page and numbered consecutively according to the symbols suggested

IDENTIFYING #_____
FULL TITLE_____

AUDIOVISUAL EVALUATION FORM
Producer_____
Date_____

DESCRIPTION (Use the appropriate items):
  FILMSTRIP:
    ____frames   ____color   ____b/w
    ____script   ____manual   ____record
    ____minutes

  RECORDINGS:
    DISC: ____16 ____33⅓ ____45
      ____78 RPM (speed)
      Size of disc:____7 ____10 ____12
      ____mono ____stereo
      ____libretto ____teaching helps

  KITS, GAMES:
    ____amount and type of pieces included

    _____

  PERIODICALS, PAMPHLETS:
    _____v. _____Date

  AGE LEVEL:_____

  SUMMARY (contents): 2 sentences, be specific

MOTION PICTURE:
  ____8 mm. ____16 mm. ____guide
  ____color ____b/w ____minutes

TAPES: cassette ____reel to reel
    ____minutes ____study helps

VIDEOTAPE: ____# of tapes ____b/w
  Size: ____¾″ ____1″ ____minutes

PICTURES, POSTERS,
PHOTOGRAPHS: ____size

SLIDES: number ____color ____b/w
  ____size (2 x 2) or _____other
  ____script

TRANSPARENCIES: ____sheets
  ____overlays _____size

RECOMMENDATION: Keep: ____yes ____no
  ____questionable ____weed
  ____historical purposes disregard because:

  _____

LOST: _____Last known date

LIBRARY RECORD

☐ Remove from accession record

☐ Pull catalog cards

☐ Remove items from storage area

☐ Remove from published listing

  Add to:_____

EVALUATION:
  Physical condition: Check for breaks, color fade.

  _____

  Content: ____dated ____incomplete
  ____clothing ____language
  ____teaching methods ____out of date
                    emphasis
  _____other

Evaluation by_____
Date_____

VI. SPECIAL COLLECTIONS

A church resource library may have a special collection of editions of the Bible, a group of old church books, a collection of objects from a period in history or objects of cultures of the world, an international doll collection, or some other collection of materials that have special meaning for the local congregation. These may come as a gift to the church, and the library is made responsible for their use and care. Use the basic steps for accessioning, classifying, and cataloging such items. Then arrange carefully for their display and/or storage.

The library is a logical place for a depository of old and current items that relate to the history of your own congregation and of your denomination. These items may be available on limited sign-out arrangements, or persons may be expected to use such old materials in the library area.

If the library has unusual items on local history, a separate collection may be developed on local history. This will vary with the library and the place it plays in the life of the congregation and the community. Being good stewards of these items now will help those who come later and who may wonder what it was like in the early days of your church or town.

If your congregation has a person designated as historian, this person should help in this project. A historical file would include newspaper clippings, copies of printed booklets, directories, bulletins, yearly reports and pictures, a review of the year, or other materials that would give clues to persons studying the events of a particular period of time.

Arrange these items in a vertical file, numbering each item and describing it on an inventory sheet. Very old items are often best stored flat. The catalog card may indicate that a file is kept and can be secured from the librarian to use for historical research. In order to serve classes preparing for church membership, a smaller file of copies should also be available. These would be available for checkout, while the originals would remain in the library for reference use only.

BIBLIOGRAPHY

Many books quickly go out of print and are hard to find. It is also difficult to keep book lists up to date. Several selected library resources are listed here along with suggestions of places to find equipment, supplies, and lists appropriate for congregational libraries.

Library Resources

Dewey, Melvil. *Abridged Dewey Decimal Classification and Relative Index,* 11th ed. Albany, N.Y.: Forest Press, 1979. ISBN 0-910608-22-9.

*————. *"200" Religion Class,* based on the 19th ed., unabridged. Nashville: Broadman Press, 1980. ISBN 0-08054-3107-1.

*Hannaford, Claudia. *The ABC's of Financing Church and Synagogue Libraries,* CSLA Guide #13, gives suggestions on budgeting, bookkeeping forms, and ideas for fund-raising. Church and Synagogue Library Association, P.O. Box 19357, Portland, Ore. 97219. ISBN 0-9-15324-23-7.

*Ling, Evelyn R. *Archives in the Church or Synagogue Library,* CSLA Guide #10, gives information on how to set up an archives, what to save, how to store items and exhibits using your items. Church and Synagogue Library Association, P.O. Box 19357, Portland, Ore. 97219. ISBN 0-915324-18-0.

*Paris, Janelle A. *Planning Bulletin Boards for Church and Synagogue Libraries,* CSLA Guide #11, gives step-by-step ideas to help you create exciting bulletin boards for your library, such as selecting a theme, planning a caption, decorations, lettering. Church and Synagogue Library Association, P.O. Box 19357, Portland, Ore. 97219. ISBN 0-915324-20-2.

Rovira, Carmen and Caroline Reyes. *Sears List of Subject Headings,* 13th ed. N.Y.: H. W. Wilson Co., 1986. ISBN 0-8242-0730-0.

*Smith, Ruth S. *Getting the Books off the Shelf,* CSLA Guide #12, gives ideas for promoting the materials by the way your library is set up, events that can be sponsored, materials created to catch the eyes of potential library users. Church and Synagogue Library Association, P.O. Box 19357, Portland, Ore. 97219. ISBN 0-915324-22-9.

Equipment and Supplies

Names and addresses of library supply houses are listed in *Church and Synagogue Library Resources,* comp. Rachel Kohl and Dorothy Rodda, 1984. ISBN 0-015324-08-3.

For computer software to make catalog cards

---

*Resources that would be useful to supplement this manual.

order *The Librarian's Helper: A Productivity Tool for Librarians*, Jennifer Pritchett and Fred Hill from Scarecrow Press, 52 Liberty Street, Metuchen, N.J. 08840. This program will help you make catalog cards, spine labels, book cards, and pocket labels. You may wish to keep a list of your books by accession number and sort by author or title. This is usable on Apple and IBM Compatibles. Write for information and a demo.

For computer supplies check with library suppliers. One is University Products, Inc., P.O. Box 101, Holyoke, Mass. 01041. In addition this company offers a variety of acid-free materials for archival storage.

For a firm covering, called "cover-ups," for paperbacks and soft-bound books, write to Janway Company, Academy Road, R.D. 3, Box 211, Cogan Station, Pa. 17728, or call collect 717-494-1239. Janway also offers good prices on T-shirts and canvas bags with silk screen library designs.

For library promotional materials send for a catalog from Upstart, Box 889, Hagerstown, Md. 21741, or call toll free 1-800-448-4887. Upstart has posters, banners, buttons, shirts, bookmarks, and other items.

Book Lists

Book lists are created for one or more purposes. The contents of the list are always colored by the person or group who compiles the list and by their special interests or concerns. Try to learn as much as you can about the source of the list, who created it, what was the purpose, what group or company is underwriting the costs and publicity.

Books and Religion is a monthly review founded by Iris and Kendig Cully at the Divinity School of Duke University, Durham, N.C. Includes previews, excerpts, and reviews of the best of the nearly two thousand new titles in religion published each year. This group also monitors four hundred scholarly publications. To get information and a sample issue or to subscribe, write to Books and Religion, P.O. Box 3000, Dept. LL, Denville, N.J. 07834.

Church and Synagogue Library Bulletin is a bimonthly containing reviews of current religious books reviewed by member librarians. The bulletin also includes articles on operating a library. For membership information write to Church and Synagogue Library Association, Dept. MJD, P.O. Box 19357, Portland, Ore. 97219. This group publishes several book lists in longer formats and many on specialized subjects at little cost. One is *Providing Reference Service in Church and Synagogue Libraries* by Jennifer Pritchett, CSLA Guide #15. ISBN 0-915324-16-1.

Provident Book Finder has helpful reviews on a wider range of topics. One helpful part is the index on the last page. This excellent resource is produced by the Mennonite Publishing House, 165 Pittsburgh Street, Scottsdale, Pa. 15683.

Large Print Books are excellent additions for persons with limited sight and for many older persons. Walker & Company is reprinting most of the inspirational classics. For a book list write to B. Walker, Walker & Company, 720 Fifth Ave., New York, N.Y. 10019.

Lists of Media

Find several companies that offer free catalogs of lists of purchase media items. Then look for rental libraries with annotated catalogs. One source is in the curriculum used in your congregation.

Source of teaching posters is Argus Communications, P.O. Box 7000, Allen, Tex. 75002, or call 1-800-527-4747.

ECU Film is an ecumenical film/video rental service that publishes an annotated catalog. Call 1-800-251-4091 or write ECU Film, 810 Twelfth Ave., South, Nashville, Tenn. 37203, for a catalog.

Mulberry Park publishes theme catalogs of visual materials such as literature, seasons, personal achievement, guidance for preschoolers through middle high school. Write to Mulberry Park, Inc., P.O. Box 4096, Dept. C 104, Englewood, Colo. 80151. Call 303-697-3618. Video cassettes are available.

Appendix I*

DEWEY SUBJECT CLASSIFICATION SYSTEM FOR CHURCH RESOURCE LIBRARIES

Choose the subject closest to the main content of the book or the price of media and use the assigned number.

000	**GENERAL WORKS**
010	Bibliographies and catalogs
020	Library and information sciences (manuals and tools)
028.1	Review of books and media
030	General encyclopedic works (reference works, English dictionaries, almanacs, atlases (or in 912) arranged by title
060.4	Robert's Rules of Order
100	**PHILOSOPHY, PSYCHOLOGY, ETHICS**
100	Philosophy
113	Cosmology (philosophy of nature)
116	Evolution
133	Parapsychology and occultism
150	Psychology (general items here, self-help for individuals use 158, see specific age groupings in 155.4-67)
155.4	Child psychology (through age 11, include siblings, adopted, foster, only child, institutional, exceptional children)
155.5	Psychology of adolescents (ages 12-20 years)
155.6	Psychology of adults (including status of women)
155.67	Psychology of adults (aged 65 and over)
158	Applied psychology (personal well-being, happiness, analysis, counseling, negotiation)
158.6	Vocational interest
170	Ethics (moral philosophy, put Christian ethics in 241)
172	Political ethics (international ethics, moral, social, war and peace, international relations)
173	Ethics of family relationships (marriage, separation, divorce, parent-child relationships, sibling relationships)
174	Economic, professional, occupational ethics (work, organ transplants, genetic engineering, right to die)
175	Ethics of recreation and leisure
176	Ethics of sex and reproduction (premarital, extramarital relations, contraception, homosexuality, prostitution, abortion)
178	Ethics of consumption (alcoholism, drugs, food, tobacco)
200	**RELIGION**
200	Religion (general works on Christian and non-Christian religions, philosophy, history of religion; use 230 for Christian beliefs)
203	Dictionaries, encyclopedias, concordances of Christianity
210	Natural religion
211	Concepts of God (polytheism, monotheism, pantheism, deism, humanism, secularism, agnosticism, skepticism, atheism)
213	Creation (of life and human life, evolution vs. creation)
215	Science and religion (technology, cybernetics, life on other worlds, space flight
218	Humankind (formerly man, place and nature in universe)
220	Bible (Holy scriptures for Judaism and Christianity)
220.3	Dictionaries and encyclopedias (concordances in 220.5)
220.4	Original texts (early versions)
220.5	Bible (texts, translations, modern versions)
220.53	Bibles in languages other than English
220.7	Bible commentaries
220.9	Bible geography/history of Bible lands and times, customs
220.92	Collected works on Bible people, biography
220.93	Bible archaeology
220.95	Bible stories retold

---

*These Dewey numbers have been selected for church libraries from the 200 Religion Class from the 19th Unabridged Dewey and the rest of the classes from the Dewey Decimal Classification, 11th Abridged ed. Consideration has been given to the appropriate numbers for children's books, i.e., infancy of Jesus 232.92, Bible stories retold in 220.95, dolphins 599.5, dinosaurs 567.9. Some numbers have been created to help sort out age-level items, i.e., CHRISTIAN EDUCATION FOR PRESCHOOL 268.431, PRAYERS FOR CHILDREN 242.682, CHRISTIAN EDUCATION—MENTALLY RETARDED 268.91, and HOLIDAYS separated into Valentine's Day, Thanksgiving.

221	Old Testament (books about the whole Bible, introductions and study guides about all or part of the Old Testament)
	Specific books of the Old Testament have their own number listed in the "200 Religion Class of Dewey"
222	Historical books of the Old Testament (Genesis–Esther)
223	Poetic books of the Old Testament (Job–Song of Solomon)
224	Prophetic books of the Old Testament (Isaiah–Malachi)
225	New Testament (general books about the New Testament) Specific books of the New Testament have their own number listed in the "200 Religion Class of Dewey"
226	Gospels and Acts (include harmonies)
227	Epistles (Romans–Jude)
228	Revelation
229	Apocrypha (intertestamental works)
230	Christian theology (Christian doctrines, beliefs, creeds, faith, humankind [man], sin, good and evil, suffering, salvation)
231	God (ways to know God and Trinity)
231.3	Holy Spirit
232	Jesus Christ
232.92	Infancy of Jesus (through the visit to the Temple at age 12)
232.94	John the Baptist
232.95	Public life of Jesus (baptism, temptation, calling of disciples, teachings, miracles, Last Supper, last words to disciples)
232.96	Passion and death of Jesus (betrayal of Judas, trial and condemnation, crucifixion, death, burial)
232.97	Resurrection, appearances, ascension of Jesus
233	Humankind (man, creation, fall, original sin, accountability, guilt, nature, image of God, child of God, body and soul, freedom of choice between good and evil)
234	Salvation and grace (faith redemption, justification, sanctification, gifts of the Holy Spirit, sacraments as a means of grace, obedience, predestination, election, free will)
236	Death (life after death, immortality, heaven, hell, purgatory, judgment, millennium, last judgment)
238	Creeds, confessions of faith, covenants, catechisms
240	Christian moral and devotional theology (conscience, sins, virtues, codes of conduct such as the Ten Commandments, Sermon on the Mount, Golden Rule)
242	Devotional literature (meditations, prayers, collections and general materials) Try to find a more specific number in this class. Place items on importance of prayer in 248.3.
242.2	Prayers and meditation for daily use (calendars of devotions)
242.3	Prayers and meditations for the whole church year
242.33	For Advent and Christmas
242.34	Lent
242.35	Holy Week
242.36	Easter
242.4	Prayers for time of illness, trouble, bereavement
242.5	Based on passages from the Bible (23rd Psalm, Sermon on the Mount)
242.6	Prayers and meditations for specific groups of persons, including family
242.682	Children
242.683	Youth
242.6834	College students
242.684	Adults, including married couples
242.6842	Men
242.6843	Women
242.685	Adults over age 65
242.7	Specific groups of prayers (Lord's Prayer, Bible prayers, thanksgiving, petition)
242.8	Collections of prayers
246	Art in Christianity (religious significance of symbols, architecture, musical and dramatic arts, for religious art see 704.9)
246.5	Symbols
247	Church furnishings
248	Personal religion (Christian experience, practice and life)
248.2	Religious experience
248.3	Worship (about worship, prayers, meditations, and methods of each)
248.4	Christian life and practice (marriage and family life)
248.6	Stewardship
249	Christian observances in family life (family prayers, ceremonies, training of children)
250	The Christian Church—the local church perspective (for history use 270)
251	Preaching
251.07	Radio and television, preaching
252	Sermons
252.53	Children's sermons
253	Clergy and pastoral duties
253.5	Counseling
254	Church administration (including government, membership, programs, buildings, equipment, grounds, public relations, church staff)
254.8	Church finance
255	Religious congregations and orders
259	Activities by the parish or religious order (i.e., specialized ministry to feed the hungry, with prisoners or with children)
260	The Christian Church (put comprehensive works here)
261	Church social theology
261.2	Christianity and other systems of belief
261.7	Christianity and political affairs

261.8	Christianity and socioeconomic problems
262	Church government (general manuals, books of policy; for church law may use 262.9)
262.1	Governing leaders of church (including laity)
262.5	General councils (ecumenical concerns, Christian unity)
262.9	Church law
263	Church year, celebrations of the church year
263.3	Sunday
263.91	Advent and Christmas
263.92	Lent and Holy Week
263.93	Easter
264	Church worship (services, ceremonies, liturgy, and ritual)
264.2	Books about music in worship (for music scores use 783)
265	Sacraments and ceremonies
265.1	Baptism
265.2	Confirmation and membership
265.3	Lord's Supper or Communion
265.5	Marriages (as a ceremony)
266	Missions
268	Christian education (theory, history, philosophy)
268.2	Buildings and equipment for Christian education
268.3	Leadership for Christian education (personnel, recruitment, training)
268.4	Christian education (administration, organization, teaching methods)
268.431	Christian education—preschool children (to age 6)
268.432	Christian education—children (ages 6-12)
268.433	Christian education—youth (ages 12-20)
268.434	Christian education—adults
268.435	Christian education—older adults
268.436	Christian education—singles
268.437	Vacation Bible or church school
268.438	Christian education—family/home
268.439	Christian education—intergenerational
268.6	Methods of teaching: how to use in church education, including art, drama, media material
268.7	Christian education services (anniversaries, teacher dedication, special days, festivals, and rallies)
268.9	Christian education—persons with special needs (general works)
268.91	Christian education—physically handicapped (including deaf and blind)
268.92	Christian education—mentally retarded
268.94	Christian education—emotionally disturbed
269	Spiritual renewal (retreats)
269.2	Evangelism
270	Church history (general church history)
270.9	Church history—local church
280	Christian denominations and sects including Protestantism

282.2	Roman Catholic churches
283	Anglican churches (including Episcopal)
284.1	Lutheran churches
285	Presbyterian churches
285.834	United Church of Christ
286	Baptist churches
287	Methodist churches
287.6	United Methodist churches
287.8	Black Methodist churches
289	Other denominations (Friends, Mennonites, Christian Science, Latter-Day Saints, Nazarene, Evangelical United Brethren, Pentecostal)
291	Comparative religion
291.9	Cults
292	Non-Christian religions
294.3	Buddhism
294.5	Hinduism
296	Judaism
297	Islam
299	Other religions (African, Confucianism, Taoism, Shintoism)

300 SOCIAL SCIENCES

301	Sociology (general works on social science and social institutions)
304.2	Pollution
304.6	Population (number of births, deaths, family size)
305	Social stratification (problems of discrimination, conflict)
305.2	Retirement
305.3	Single
305.4	Widowed
305.8	Racial, ethnic, national groups
306.7	Courtship, dating
306.8	Marriage (or use 248.4)
327	International relations
330	Economics
333	Land economics (natural resources)
333.7	Use of natural resources
335	Socialism and related systems
335.43	Communism
360	Social problems (crime, prisons, welfare, poverty, disasters)
361.7	Volunteerism
362.1	Physical illness (terminal care)
362.2	Mental and emotional illnesses (including alcoholism, drug addiction)
362.3	Mental retardation
362.4	Problems of and services to the physically handicapped
362.5	Poverty
362.6	Problems of and services to adults aged 65 plus, see also elderly abuse
362.7	Problems and services to young people (through age 17, including day-care services, aid to dependent children, foster care, adoption, child abuse, runaway children and teens)

362.8	Other groups (families, women, racial, ethnic, veterans)
363.7	Environmental problems and services (pollution, waste, noise)
363.8	Hunger
363.9	Population problems
369	Miscellaneous kinds of associations
369.43	Boy Scouts
369.463	Girl Scouts
370	Education
371.4	Vocational guidance (see 253 for ministry as a vocation)
372	Elementary education (including nursery school)
373	Secondary education
374	Adult education
378	Higher education (including college catalogs)
384	Telecommunication
384.54	Radio
384.55	Television (closed circuit, cable)
384.6	Telephony (computer communications using telephone lines, teleconferencing)
387	Water, air, space transportation
388	Ground transportation
390	Customs, etiquette, folklore
392	Weddings
394	General customs (games, toys, dances, pageants, parades, ceremonies, and observances)
394.2	Special occasions (general book of several holidays, church holidays use 263)
394.3	Halloween
394.4	Presidents holidays
394.5	Thanksgiving
394.6	Valentine's Day
394.7	May be assigned to specific holidays
394.8	May be assigned to specific holidays
394.9	May be assigned to specific holidays
395	Etiquette (manners)
398	Folklore
398.2	Fairy tales, ghost stories, heroes (for religious mythology use 291.1)

400	**LANGUAGE**
423	English language dictionaries
430	German language (use 433 for dictionary)
440	French (use 443 for dictionary)
461	Spanish (use 463 for dictionary)
492.4	Hebrew language dictionaries
495.1	Chinese
495.6	Japanese
495.7	Korean
495.9	Thai and Vietnamese

500	**PURE SCIENCES**
500	Natural sciences (natural history and comprehensive works on pure and applied sciences)
508	Travel and surveys

520	Astronomy
523.2	Solar system
523.3	Moon
523.7	Sun
523.8	Stars
525	Earth
529	Time (calendars)
537	Electricity
538	Magnetism
539	Physics
540	Chemistry
550	Sciences of the earth and other worlds
551	Geology
551.6	Climatology and weather
552	Rocks
560	Paleontology (fossils)
567.9	Dinosaurs
570	Life sciences
572	Human race
573	Physical anthropology
574	Biology
574.4	Anatomy
574.5	Ecology (food chains, environments)
575	Organic evolution and genetics
581	Botany
591	Zoology
594	Shells
595	Worms, lobsters, crabs, shrimps
595.4	Spiders
595.7	Insects (dragonflies, grasshoppers)
595.76	Beetles (ladybugs, fireflies)
595.78	Butterflies, moths
597	Fishes
597.9	Reptiles
597.92	Turtles
597.95	Lizards
597.96	Snakes
598	Birds
599	Mammals
599.2	Marsupials (kangaroos, opossums)
599.32	Rabbits, mice, porcupines, squirrels
599.5	Dolphins, whales
599.6	Elephants
599.72	Horses, rhinoceroses
599.73	Bisons, camels, deer, otters, raccoons, seals, walruses
599.8	Primates (baboons, apes, monkeys)

600	**TECHNOLOGY (applied sciences)**
610	Medicine
612	Human physiology (functions, biochemistry, reproduction, development, maturation, sex education)
613	General and personal hygiene (inherited diseases, personal cleanliness, clothing, cosmetics as factors in health)
613.2	Dietetics (weight-gain-and-loss programs)
613.7	Physical fitness (exercise, posture, rest, sleep)
613.8	Addictions (use of alcoholic beverages, drugs, tobacco)

613.9	Family planning and sex hygiene (including birth control)
614	Public health and safety
615	Drugs and medical advisers
616	Diseases
616.02	First aid
616.8	Alzheimer's Disease
616.86	Addictions to alcohol, drugs, tobacco
621	Applied physics (how machines operate, including heat and electricity)
625	Engineering (railroads and roads)
629.1	Aerospace engineering (aircraft and airports)
629.4	Astronautics (space flight)
635	Gardens (general and vegetable)
635.9	Flower gardens (ornamentals)
640	Home economics and family living (management of home, personal life, money and budgets)
641	Food and drink
641.1	Nutrition (relation to one's health use 613.2)
641.5	Cookery (cookbooks of all kinds)
645	Furnishings and home decorating
646	Sewing, clothing
646.7	Management of personal and family living (grooming, charm, dating, behavior, choice of mate, family living, guides for adults aged 65, i.e., retirement guides)
649	Child rearing, home care of sick
649.8	Hospices
651	Business and office skills (communications, data processing, records, accounting, teleconferencing)

700 THE ARTS

700	Art (general works on fine and decorative arts, art appreciation, art history; use 704.9 for religious art, 246 for art and Christianity)
704.9	Art—Religious
708	Museums and collections, catalogs of (can be separated by countries)
720	Architecture
726	Church or religious architecture
730	Sculpture
741	Drawing
745	Decorative arts (color, antiques, design, folk arts, flower arranging)
745.5	Handicraft (arts and crafts, creative activities; use 268.6 for use of crafts in church education)
745.6	Lettering (calligraphy, illuminated manuscripts)
746.4	Needle handwork and weaving
750	Painting
760	Graphic arts (posters, prints)
770	Photography
780	Music
783	Sacred music
783.9	Hymns

784.6	Songs for special groups, including children
790.1	Recreation (leisure, games, hobbies, sports)
791.3	Clowns
791.5	Puppets
792	Theater
792.1	Religious drama
793	Indoor games and amusements
796	Outdoor sports and games (for hiking and camping use 796.5)
796.5	Hiking and camping

800 LITERATURE

800	Literature (anthologies, collections)
808.5	Public speaking (storytelling, choral speaking)
808.7	Anecdotes
810	American literature
811	Poetry
812	Drama, texts of plays (use 792 for helps in presenting dramas)
814	Essays
815	Speeches and addresses
817	Satire and humor
818	Other types of literature (diaries, quotations, journals)
860	Spanish literature
895.1	Chinese literature
895.6	Japanese literature
895.7	Korean literature
895.9	Thai and Vietnamese literature
F or FIC	Fiction arranged by author in one section

900 HISTORY AND GEOGRAPHY AND BIOGRAPHY

909	General world history
910	General geography (comprehensive works, including exploration and discovery)
910.2	World travel guides (may be placed by name of country)
912	Atlases, maps
920	Biography (may use B and arrange alphabetically by name of biographee)
922	Biography of religious leaders, thinkers, and workers
930	History of the ancient world to A.D. 500, including archaeology
932	Ancient Egypt
933	Ancient Palestine
935	Ancient Mesopotamia (including Babylonian Empire)
937	Ancient Italian Peninsula and adjacent territory
938	Ancient Greece
940	Western Europe
941	British Isles (942 England and Wales)
943	Central Europe (Germany)
944	France

945	Italy
946	Spain
947	Eastern Europe (including the Soviet Union)
948	Northern Europe (including Scandinavia)
949	Other parts of Europe (Netherlands, Low Countries, Switzerland, Greece, Balkans, Yugoslavia)
950	Asia and the Far East
951	China
952	Japan
953	Arabian Peninsula (Arab states)
954	South Asia (including India, Pakistan, and Bangladesh)
956	Middle East (including Israel, Palestine, and Jordan)
959	Southeast Asia
960	Africa
962	Egypt and Sudan
963	Ethiopia
964	Northwest Africa
965	Algeria
966	West Africa and Islands
967	Central Africa
968	Southern Africa
970	General history of North America
971	Canada
972	Mexico and Middle Americas
973	United States
974–979	Specific states of United States
980	South America
990	Oceania
993	New Zealand
994	Australia

APPENDIX II SUBJECT HEADINGS

You will note that the words used in the Dewey listing are not always the same words that are used as subject headings. You will also find that there are some subject headings given in the CIP (cataloging in publication; see page in text) that will not agree with the subject headings listed here.

The reasons for these differences are: There are two organizations working on listings (Sears and Library of Congress); there are a variety of ways of saying the same thing in our language; and there are some regional emphases or common usages that may not appear in either of these systems.

In this resource, we have taken the common items that are used in Christian education resource centers and have tried to give a broad spread of subjects or topics to which you may add others when you have a need for them.

Make additional appropriate subject headings for:

1. Proper names, for example, LUTHER, MARTIN, or NEW YORK

2. Names of associations, societies, clubs, institutions

3. Common names for animals, birds, fishes, flowers, foods, games

It is possible also to identify the content of a book or a piece of media by adding to the proper name or common name other words after a long dash—such as:

FIRST UNITED METHODIST
CHURCH—DIRECTORIES
FIRST UNITED METHODIST
CHURCH—HISTORY, 1900
FIRST UNITED METHODIST
CHURCH—HISTORY, 1950
FIRST UNITED METHODIST
CHURCH—YEARBOOKS
BIBLE—BIBLIOGRAPHY
BIBLE—DRAMA
BIBLE—FICTION
BIBLE—MAPS
BIBLE—PERIODICALS
BIBLE—POETRY
BIBLE—QUOTATIONS
BIBLE—SOCIAL LIFE AND CUSTOMS

Any of these could be used to help users find the appropriate material. As subject headings, they are capitalized on the first line of the card.

You will find some of these useful to identify books, kits, or media for mission education, social life and customs (following the name of a country). Example, INDIA—MISSION EDUCATION; INDIA—SOCIAL LIFE AND CUSTOMS.

Do not be discouraged about the potential number of subject headings. Choose the number of subject headings that will help library users make the best use of the materials that are in the library.

Keep a list of the subject headings that you have used in a card file, put one subject heading on each card, and file the cards alphabetically. As you catalog materials, refer to this list and try to use the same headings. When you add another new heading, make a card for it and add it to the file.

Another way to keep track of the subject headings used is to put a check mark by the items in this resource list and add each new subject heading when used. This list will be current with the subjects that are in your file.

Though a piece of media can have more than one Dewey number, when the final decision is made and the number is given, the item can be put in only one place on the shelf. Several topics can be dealt with in the media piece; a subject card for each topic will help persons know the contents of the resources. The next question is usually, How many subject cards are needed? As many as *you* need, to identify the main subjects covered in the piece that you are cataloging.

Work from the more general topic if the coverage is general to the more specific if it is specific. For example, the topic "aging" is more than retirement, elderly, or some of the unique problems such as elderly abuse, elderly care, or older adults. Ask the question, What is the material really about? Then choose the best Dewey number and the best subject headings.

A

ABORTION. See also SEXUAL ETHICS	176
Abuse. See CHILD ABUSE 362.7, ELDERLY ABUSE 362.6	
Accidents—Prevention. See PUBLIC HEALTH AND SAFETY	614
Acting. See DRAMA, RELIGIOUS DRAMA 792.1	792
ADDICTIONS	616.86
Administration. See CHRISTIAN EDUCATION—ADMINISTRATION AND ORGANIZATION	268.4
ADOLESCENCE, PSYCHOLOGY OF	155.5
Adults, Older. See CHRISTIAN EDUCATION—OLDER ADULTS	268.435
Adults. See CHRISTIAN EDUCATION—ADULTS	268.434
ADULTS, PSYCHOLOGY OF	155.6
ADVENT, CHRISTMAS	263.91
AERONAUTICS (including space travel)	629.1
AFRICA	960
AGED, PSYCHOLOGY OF. See also ELDERLY	155.67

AGRICULTURE (indoor and outdoor gardening) — 635 or 635.9

ALCOHOLISM, TOBACCO, DRUGS, FOOD, USE AND ABUSE OF — 178

ALMANACS — 030

ANATOMY. See also LIFE SCIENCES — 574.4

ANECDOTES (illustrations) — 808.7

ANIMALS. See ZOOLOGY — 590

Anthologies. See LITERATURE — 800

ANTHROPOLOGY (study of humankind). See also LIFE SCIENCES — 573

ANTIQUES — 745

Apocrypha. See BIBLE–APOCRYPHA–VERSION–DATE — 220.53

ARCHAEOLOGY. See also BIBLICAL–ARCHAEOLOGY — 220.93

ARCHITECTURE — 720

Art in Christianity. See CHRISTIAN ART AND SYMBOLISM — 246

ART (general works in fine and decorative arts, art appreciation, art history; see 246 for CHRISTIAN ART AND SYMBOLISM) — 700

ART IN CHURCH EDUCATION (methods of instruction) — 268.6

ARTS AND CRAFTS (including creative activities, how-to guides; see 268.6 for use in church education) — 745.5

ASIA AND THE FAR EAST — 950

ATLASES (or use 912) — 030

AUDIOVISUAL MATERIALS — 268.6

Autobiographies. See BIOGRAPHY — 920 or B

B

BAPTISM — 265.1

BAPTISTS — 286

Beliefs. See THEOLOGY — 230

BIBLE (text of the whole Bible, modern versions, and translations) — 220.5

BIBLE—APOCRYPHA — 229

BIBLE—ARCHAEOLOGY — 220.93

BIBLE—COMMENTARIES (single or multi-volume sets) — 220.7

BIBLE—CONCORDANCES — 220.5

BIBLE—DICTIONARIES — 220.3

Bible—Encyclopedias. See BIBLE—DICTIONARIES — 220.3

BIBLE—GEOGRAPHY — 220.9

BIBLE—HISTORY — 220.9

Bible—Introductions (books about the whole Bible). See BIBLE STUDY — 220

BIBLE—NEW TESTAMENT (introductions, study guides, commentaries, books about all or parts of the New Testament) — 225

BIBLE—OLD TESTAMENT (introductions, study guides, commentaries, books about all or parts of the Old Testament) — 221

BIBLE—SOCIAL LIFE AND CUSTOMS — 220.9

BIBLE—STORIES — 220.95

BIBLE—STUDY. See 220 for the whole Bible, 221 for Old Testament study guides, and 225 for New Testament — 220

Bible versions. See BIBLE — 220.5

Bibliographies. See BIBLIOGRAPHY (SUBJECT) — 010

BIOGRAPHY (collections or individuals) — 920 or B

BIOGRAPHY OF RELIGIOUS LEADERS — 922

BIOLOGY — 574

BIRDS — 598

BIRTH CONTROL. See also SEXUAL ETHICS — 176

BOTANY (plants, identification and care of) — 581

BUILDINGS (and equipment for Christian education) — 268.2

C

Cable television. See TELECOMMUNICATION — 384.55

CAMPING — 796.5

CATALOGS — 010

CATHOLIC CHURCH — 282.2

CELEBRATIONS OF THE CHURCH YEAR (Advent, Christmas, Epiphany, Lent, Easter, Pentecost) — 263

CENTRAL AMERICA — 972

Ceremonies. See SACRAMENTS or the specific sacrament, as BAPTISM 265.1 — 265

CHILD ABUSE — 362.7

CHILD STUDY (psychology of all children through age 11, including adopted, foster, institutionalized, exceptional) — 155.4

CHILD WELFARE (works on aid, support, and protection of children by the state or private welfare organizations) — 362.7

CHILDREN. See also CHRISTIAN EDUCATION—CHILDREN AGES 6-12 — 268.432

Children's books. See juvenile literature, section marked J; or books for young children, section marked E

CHILDREN'S SERMONS — 252.53

CHILDREN'S SONGS — J784 or 784

CHORAL SPEAKING (including verse choirs) — 808.5

Christ. See JESUS CHRIST — 232

CHRISTIAN ART AND SYMBOLISM — 246

Christian church. See DISCIPLES OF CHRIST as a denomination — 286.6

Christian denominations and SECTS
(use the particular name of the
denomination and Dewey number
280–289)

Christian doctrines. See THEOLOGY — 230

CHRISTIAN EDUCATION (theology,
history, philosophy) — 268

CHRISTIAN EDUCATION
(administration and organization) — 268.4

CHRISTIAN EDUCATION—ADULTS — 268.434

CHRISTIAN EDUCATION—
CHILDREN (ages 6-12) — 268.432

CHRISTIAN EDUCATION—
EMOTIONALLY DISTURBED — 268.94

CHRISTIAN EDUCATION—
FAMILY/HOME — 268.438

CHRISTIAN EDUCATION—
INTERGENERATIONAL — 268.439

CHRISTIAN EDUCATION—
MENTALLY RETARDED — 268.92

CHRISTIAN EDUCATION—OLDER
ADULTS — 268.435

CHRISTIAN EDUCATION—
PERSONS WITH SPECIAL NEEDS — 268.9

CHRISTIAN EDUCATION—
PHYSICALLY HANDICAPPED
(including deaf and blind) — 268.91

CHRISTIAN EDUCATION—
PRESCHOOL CHILDREN (to age 6) — 268.431

Christian education recruitment and
personnel. See LEADERSHIP — 268.3

CHRISTIAN EDUCATION—YOUTH — 268.433

CHRISTIAN LIFE — 248

Christian symbolism. See CHRISTIAN
ART AND SYMBOLISM — 246.5

CHRISTIAN UNITY (ecumenical
concerns, NCC, COCU) — 262.5

CHRISTIANITY — 201

Christianity–social theology. See
CHURCH HISTORY—MODERN
(attitudes of Christianity toward and
influence on secular matters) — 261

CHRISTIANITY AND CIVIL
GOVERNMENT (and politics) — 261.7

CHRISTIANITY AND ECONOMIC
PROBLEMS — 261.8

CHRISTIANITY AND OTHER
RELIGIONS — 261.2

CHRISTMAS. See also ADVENT — 263.91

CHURCH (general works, including
nature of the church) — 260

CHURCH ADMINISTRATION
(trustees, deacons, property, ruling
body) — 254

Church and social problems. See
CHURCH HISTORY—MODERN or
20TH CENTURY — 261

CHURCH ARCHITECTURE — 726

CHURCH FINANCE — 254.8

CHURCH GOVERNMENT (general
books and manuals, books of policy,

and church records). See also
CHURCH LAW — 262

CHURCH GROUPS (prayer groups,
special interest groups; for Christian
education see 268 and the number
following) — 259

CHURCH HISTORY (may use periods
of time, e.g., HISTORY—MIDDLE
AGES: EARLY CHURCH or 20TH
CENTURY. May also use specific
place or area as UNITED STATES—
CHURCH HISTORY) — 270

CHURCH LAW — 262.9

CHURCH—LOCAL (general items and
may include books of sermons or
classify with the subject) — 250

CHURCH MUSIC (in worship) See also
HYMNS — 264.2

Church worship. See WORSHIP — 264

Church year. See CELEBRATIONS OF
THE CHURCH YEAR — 263

CITIZENSHIP (duties and obligations) — 323

College catalogs. See EDUCATION,
HIGHER — 378

Commentaries. See BIBLE—
COMMENTARIES — 220.7

Communion. See LORD'S SUPPER or
SACRAMENTS — 265.3

Comparative religions. See
CHRISTIANITY AND OTHER
RELIGIONS — 291

CONFIRMATION — 265.2

Cookbooks. See COOKERY — 640

COUNSELING (pastoral) — 253.5

Crafts. See ARTS AND CRAFTS — 745.5

CREATIVE ACTIVITIES — 268.6

CREEDS. See also THEOLOGY — 238 or 230

CULTS — 291.9

Customs, Bible. See BIBLE—SOCIAL
LIFE AND CUSTOMS — 220.9

D

DATING. See also Christian marriage
284.4 — 306.7

DAY CARE — 362.7

DEAD SEA SCROLLS — 221.4

DEATH (preparation for, acceptance of) — 236

DECORATIVE ARTS (including color,
interior design, floral arts, antiques) — 745

Denominations. See SECTS and
individual denominations — 280

DEVOTIONAL LITERATURE
(including family worship resources) — 242

Dictionaries—Bible. See
BIBLE—DICTIONARIES — 200.3

Dictionaries—English language. See
ENGLISH LANGUAGE—
DICTIONARIES — 030

Dictionaries—foreign languages. See 400
    class for the number, i.e.,
    SPANISH—DICTIONARIES 463
DINOSAURS 567.9
DIVORCE 173
DRAMA (including stage presentations,
    lighting, sets, makeup, acting; for use
    in Christian education see 268.6) 792
DRAMA IN EDUCATION (in Christian
    education) 268.6
DRAMA (texts of play). See 792 for
    helps in presenting dramas 812
DRUG ABUSE 178 or 613.8

E

EARTH SCIENCES (geology, weather,
    rocks, fossils) 550
EASTER. See also LENT, HOLY WEEK 263.93
Easy reading and picture books through
    grade 2 E
ECOLOGY (interrelation of organisms
    and environment) 574.5
ECONOMICS 330
Ecumenical concerns. See CHRISTIAN
    UNITY 262.5
EDUCATION. See 268 for Christian
    Education 370
EDUCATION, HIGHER (including
    college catalogs) 378
EGYPT (ancient Egypt 932) 962
ELDERLY 155.67
ELDERLY ABUSE 362.6
ENCYCLOPEDIAS 030
Environment. See ECOLOGY 574.5
Episcopal church. See PROTESTANT
    EPISCOPAL CHURCH IN THE USA 283
ETHICS 170
Ethics of family life. See FAMILY LIFE 173
Ethics, sexual. See SEXUAL ETHICS 176
ETIQUETTE 395
Europe. See CENTRAL EUROPE 943,
    EASTERN EUROPE 947,
    NORTHERN EUROPE 948,
    WESTERN EUROPE 940
EVANGELISM 269.2

F

Faith. See THEOLOGY 230
Family. See CHRISTIAN
    EDUCATION— FAMILY 268.438
FAMILY LIFE (ethics of, including
    marriage, divorce, responsibility of,
    parents) 173
Family planning, sex instruction. See
    SEX EDUCATION 612
Family worship resources. See
    DEVOTIONAL LITERATURE 242.6
FICTION F
Film making. See PHOTOGRAPHY 770
FIRST AID. See also PUBLIC
    HEALTH AND SAFETY 614

FLOWER ARRANGEMENT 745
FOLKLORE (mythology, fairy tales) 398
Foreign language dictionaries. See
    DICTIONARIES—FOREIGN
    LANGUAGE; see 400 for the
    language

G

GAMES, SPORTS, AND RECREATION 790
Gardening, indoor and outdoor. See
    AGRICULTURE 635 or 635.9
General reference works (dictionaries,
    almanacs, encyclopedias, arranged by
    title or R) 030
GEOGRAPHY. See also HISTORY
    (general works and specific areas of
    the world) 910
GRAPHIC ARTS (posters, prints) 760
GOD (including TRINITY) 231
Good and evil. See THEOLOGY 230

H

HALLOWEEN 394.3
Handicapped persons. See CHRISTIAN
    EDUCATION—PHYSICALLY
    HANDICAPPED 268.01
MENTALLY RETARDED 268.92
EMOTIONALLY DISTURBED 268.94
Handicraft. See ARTS AND CRAFTS
    or CREATIVE ACTIVITIES 745.5
Higher education. See EDUCATION,
    HIGHER 378
HISTORY 909
History of Bible lands. See BIBLE—
    HISTORY 220.9
History of humankind. See LIFE
    SCIENCES 570
HOBBIES 790.13
HOLIDAYS (general use; see specific
    holidays such as VALENTINE'S DAY,
    THANKSGIVING, HALLOWEEN;
    see 263 for CELEBRATIONS OF
    THE CHURCH YEAR such as
    CHRISTMAS, EASTER; may also use
    holiday name) 394.2
Holy Bible. See BIBLE—VERSION
    (name of version here, i.e., REVISED
    STANDARD) 220.5
Holy Communion. See LORD'S SUPPER
    or SACRAMENTS 265.3
HOLY SPIRIT 231.3
Holy Week and Easter. See LENT,
    HOLY WEEK, EASTER 263, 263.92,
    263.93
HOME ECONOMICS 640
Homosexuality. See SEXUAL ETHICS 176
HOSPICES 362.1
Human body. See LIFE SCIENCES 570
HUMOR (type of writing) 817
HUNGER 363.8
HYMNS 783.9

I

Indians. See NATIVE AMERICANS
(may also use INDIANS OF NORTH
AMERICA or the names of tribes)   940.004
INFANTS   155.4
INSECTS   595.7
Intergenerational groups. See
CHRISTIAN EDUCATION—
INTERGENERATIONAL   268.439
Interior design. See DECORATIVE
ARTS   745
International ethics (moral and social
aspects, peace, war). See ETHICS   172
ISLAM   297
ISRAEL. See also PALESTINE   956

J

JESUS CHRIST   232
JESUS CHRIST—ART   704.9
JESUS CHRIST—INFANCY   232.92
JESUS CHRIST—CRUCIFIXION   232.96
JOHN THE BAPTIST   232.94
JUDAISM   296
Juveniles (resources for children through
grade 6)   J

L

LAITY   262
LANGUAGE AND LANGUAGES. See
specific languages in 400 class
LEADERSHIP (personnel, recruitment,
and training in Christian education)   268.3
LEISURE   790.1
LENT, HOLY WEEK, AND EASTER   263.92 or 93
LIBRARY (manuals, guides)   020
LIFE SCIENCES (history of humankind,
anatomy, human body)   570
LITERATURE—ANTHOLOGIES,
COLLECTIONS   800
LITERATURE—OTHER TYPES
(essays, letters, satire, humor)   818
Local congregation church history. See
CHURCH HISTORY—LOCAL
CONGREGATIONS, name or church
name—HISTORY   270.9
LORD'S SUPPER   265.3
LUTHERAN CHURCH   284.1

M

MAN. Use HUMANKIND. See also
THEOLOGY   230
MARRIAGE (as a ceremony)   265.5
Marriage. See FAMILY LIFE   173
MEDICAL ETHICS   174
Membership cultivation. See
EVANGELISM   254
Mentally retarded persons. See
CHRISTIAN EDUCATION—
MENTALLY RETARDED   268.92

METHODIST (general books and early
history, Wesleyan and other materials,
early history of uniting denominations
in 287). See also UNITED
METHODIST CHURCH 287.6 from
1968 to date   287
Methods of instruction. See ART IN
CHRISTIAN EDUCATION,
AUDIOVISUAL EDUCATION,
MATERIALS, DRAMA—STUDY
AND TEACHING, TEACHING
MIDDLE EAST   956
MINISTRY, CHRISTIAN (ordained,
licensed, commissioned, functions,
training; Christian vocations,
specialized ministries, lay ministries)   253
MISSIONARIES   922
MISSION EDUCATION (classify by
authors here or by geographical area
as listed in the 900s, i.e. MISSION
EDUCATION—AFRICA)
MISSIONS (general works on missions)   266
MISSIONS—COUNTRY (i.e.,
MISSIONS— CHINA)
MINORITIES (minority groups, rights,
problems)   323.1
MUSIC IN WORSHIP. See also
CHURCH MUSIC 783   264.2
MUSIC (general compositions). See 783
for sacred music   780
MYTHOLOGY. See also FOLKLORE   398

N

NATURAL RELIGION   210
NATURAL RESOURCES   333
NATURE   500
Nature of the church. See CHURCH   260
Nature study. See EARTH SCIENCE,
LIFE SCIENCES, BIOLOGY,
ECOLOGY, POLLUTION, BOTANY,
ZOOLOGY   500
Negro Methodist Churches   287.5
New Testament. See BIBLE—NEW
TESTAMENT   225
Non–Christian religions. See
RELIGIONS or indicate the individual
name as BUDDHISM, ISLAM,
JUDAISM
NORTH AMERICAN   970
NURSERY SCHOOLS. See also
CHRISTIAN EDUCATION—
PRESCHOOL 268.431   372
NUTRITION   641.1

O

OCCULT SCIENCES   133
Older adults. See CHRISTIAN
EDUCATION—OLDER ADULTS   268.435
Old Testament. See BIBLE—OLD
TESTAMENT   221

Other denominations. See FRIENDS,
  MENNONITES   289

P

PALESTINE. See HOLY LAND,
  ISRAEL   220.9, 933,
                                           956
PAINTING (including individual
  paintings)   750
Parapsychology. See OCCULTISM   133
PARENT AND CHILD. See also
  FAMILY LIFE   173
PARTIES   793
PEACE. See also ETHICS   172
Personnel—recruitment and training for
  Christian education. See
  LEADERSHIP   268.3
Persons with special needs. See
  CHRISTIAN EDUCATION—
  PERSONS WITH SPECIAL NEEDS   268.9
PETS. See ZOOLOGY for all animals   590
PHILOSOPHY   100
PHOTOGRAPHY (film making, storage)   770
PICTURE BOOKS FOR CHILDREN   E
PLAY. See also RECREATION   790.1
PLANTS. See AGRICULTURE for
  gardening helps   580
POETRY   811
POLITICAL SCIENCE   320
POLLUTION   304.2
POPULATION   304.6
Posters. See GRAPHIC ARTS   760
POVERTY   362.5
PRAYER (books about prayer; for
  collections use 242.8; see prayers for
  individual groups, i.e., YOUTH
  PRAYERS 242.683)   242
Prayer groups. See CHURCH GROUPS   259
PRESBYTERIAN CHURCH   285
PRESIDENTS HOLIDAYS   354.4
PROTESTANTISM. See also SECTS   280
PSYCHOLOGY. See age groups and
  add PSYCHOLOGY, i.e.,   150
  CHILD PSYCHOLOGY,   155.4
  AGING—PSYCHOLOGY   155.67
PASTORAL PSYCHOLOGY. See also
  COUNSELING   253.5
PUBLIC HEALTH AND SAFETY
  (including accident prevention, first
  aid)   614
PUPPETS   791.5
Psychology, child. See CHILD
  PSYCHOLOGY   155.4
PSYCHOLOGY   150

Q

Quakers. See SOCIETY OF FRIENDS   289.6
QUOTATIONS   808.8

R

RACE RELATIONS   305.8
RADIO   384.54

RECREATION. See also GAMES AND
  SPORTS, HOBBIES   790.1
Recruitment and personnel for Christian
  education. See LEADERSHIP   268.3
RELIGION (general works on Christian
  and non–Christian religions,
  philosophy, history). See 230 for
  Christian beliefs and doctrine,
  THEOLOGY   200
RELIGION AND SCIENCE   215
RELIGIONS (any name may be used
  for a subject heading, i.e.,
  CONFUCIANISM)
RELIGIOUS EDUCATION (this term
  may be used instead of CHRISTIAN
  EDUCATION with the same
  categories)
REPTILES   597.9
RETIREMENT. See also 155.67   305.2
RIGHT TO DIE   174
ROMAN CATHOLIC CHURCH   282.2
RUNAWAY CHILDREN   362.7

S

SACRAMENTS   265
Sacred Music. See CHURCH MUSIC   264.2 or 783
Safety. See PUBLIC HEALTH AND
  SAFETY   614
SALVATION. See THEOLOGY   234
Science and religion. See RELIGION
  AND SCIENCE   215
SEASONS. Add specific names such as
  AUTUMN, if desired   525
SECTS (Christian denominations)   280
SENSES. Add specific names, SMELL,
  TASTE, TOUCH, HEARING   152.1, 612
SERMON ON THE MOUNT. See also
  DEVOTIONS 242.5   226.9
SERMONS. See specific subjects, as
  LORD'S SUPPER—SERMONS   252
SEWING   640
SEX EDUCATION   612
SEXUAL ETHICS (birth control,
  abortion, homosexuality)   176
SIN. See also THEOLOGY   170
SINGLE PEOPLE   155.6 or 305.3
Social problems and the church. See
  CHURCH AND SOCIAL
  PROBLEMS (crime, prisons, welfare,
  poverty, disasters)   261.8 or 360
SOCIALISM (and related systems)   335
SOCIETY OF FRIENDS (Quakers)   289.6
SOCIOLOGY   301
SOUTH AMERICA   980
Space travel. See SPACE FLIGHT   629.4
SPIDERS   595.4
SPORTS. See also GAMES,
  RECREATION   796
STEWARDSHIP   248.6

SUFFERING. See also THEOLOGY   230
SUNDAY SCHOOL. See also
   CHRISTIAN EDUCATION and the
   specific age groups
Symbolism. See CHRISTIAN ART AND
   SYMBOLISM   246.5

T

TEACHING (art and method of)   268.6
TELECOMMUNICATION (radio,
   television, cable, video, computer)   384
TELECONFERENCING   384.6 or 651.7
TELEVISION   384
TERMINAL CARE   362.1 or 649.8
THANKSGIVING   394.5
THEOLOGY (Christian doctrines,
   beliefs, creeds, faith, man, humankind,
   good and evil, suffering, salvation)   230
TOBACCO   178
Training for Christian Education. See
   LEADERSHIP   268.3
TRAVEL   910.2
TRINITY   231

U

UNITED CHURCH OF CHRIST   285.8
UNITED METHODIST CHURCH   287.6
UNITED STATES   973
UNITED STATES—CHURCH
   HISTORY—NORTH AMERICA   277

V

VACATION BIBLE OR CHURCH
   SCHOOL   268.437

VALENTINE'S DAY   394.6
VIDEOTAPES   384
VOCATIONAL GUIDANCE. For
   ministry see 253   371.4
Vocations. See MINISTRY   253
VOLUNTEERISM   361.7

W

War. See ETHICS   172
WEDDINGS   392
Weekday preschool—nursery and
   kindergarten. See CHRISTIAN
   EDUCATION—PRESCHOOL
   CHILDREN   268.431
Welfare. See SOCIAL PROBLEMS   360
WIDOWS   305.4
World relief. See POVERTY   362.5
WORSHIP   264

Y

YOUNG ADULTS (ages 18-35). See
   CHRISTIAN
   EDUCATION—ADULTS   268.436
Young children. See CHRISTIAN
   EDUCATION—PRESCHOOL
   CHILDREN 268.431 or CHILDREN
   268.432
YOUTH. See CHRISTIAN
   EDUCATION— YOUTH   268.433
Youth psychology. See ADOLESCENT
   PSYCHOLOGY   155.5

Z

ZOOLOGY   591

APPENDIX III
HEADINGS FOR A PICTURE FILE AND FLANNEL BOARD

Bible: Creation, Beginnings
Creation
Noah
Adam

Bible: Abraham through Joseph
Abraham
Joseph
Esau
Jacob
Isaac

Bible: Moses, Joshua, Judges
Moses
Sampson
Deborah
Ten Commandments
Samuel
Joshua
Miriam
Eli
Gideon
Ruth

Bible: Kings and Prophets
Saul
Jeremiah
Amos
David
Nehemiah
Isaiah
Hezekiah
Daniel
Jonah
Esther
Elijah
Jonathan
Ezekiel
Hosea
Solomon
Ezra
Micah
Josiah
Huldah

Bible: Jesus' Nativity and Childhood
Annunciation
Life in Nazareth
Birth events
Trip to Temple
Presentation in the Temple
Flight to Egypt

Bible: Jesus' Ministry
Baptism

Temptations
Relationships with others
Teaching, preaching
Prayer
Healing
With children
Portraits and sculpture
With disciples

Bible: Jesus' Parables and Teachings
Good Samaritan
Prodigal Son
Lost Sheep
House built on rock
Widow's gift
Lost Coin
Hidden Treasure
Sower
Pharisee and publican

Bible: Jesus, Holy Week to Ascension
Visit to Bethany
Crucifixion
Betrayal
Cleansing the Temple
Walk to Emmaus
Trial
Gethsemane
Triumphal entry
Resurrection
Peter's denial
Last Supper
Ascension

Bible: Early Church
Disciples
Worship and fellowship
Women
Barnabas
Epistles
Paul
Stephen
Ministry and service
Timothy

Bible: History of
Oral tradition
Distribution
Translation
Canonization
Facsimiles
Scribes, copyists
Early writings

Archaeology
Printing

Bible: Lands and Customs
Festivals and celebrations
Synagogue
Music and psalms
Homes, family life
Villages
Jerusalem, Temple
Geography
Transportation
Occupations

Bible: Maps, Charts, Games
Maps
Games
Reference cards
Charts to aid use of Bible
Time lines

Bible: Present-Day Use
Congregational use
Family use
Individual reading

Church: Celebrations
Historical observances
Symbols
Contemporary observances
Advent
Christmas
Caroling
Posada
Epiphany
Pentecost
Feats of the Three Kings
Dramas
Lent
Palm Sunday
Holy Thursday
Good Friday
Easter

Church: Community
Confirmation
Prayer
Meeting places
Music and arts
Funerals
Fellowship
Sacraments
Weddings

Church History
In the Roman Empire

Church leaders
Denominational history
Reformation
In the Middle Ages
Ecumenical movement

Church: Ministry, Service, Witness
Church workers
Community activities
Ethnic Minority Concerns
Healing, hospitals
Hunger Concerns
Ministry of laity
Social Concerns
Witness

Church: Mission and World Concerns
Global activities
Nuclear power
Peace
Missionaries
United Nations
Special ministries

Church School: Younger Children
Sunday church school
Weekday groups
Vacation school
Infants, Toddlers
Two-year-olds
Ages 3-4
Ages 4-6

Church School: Elementary Children
Sunday church school
Weekday activities
Vacation school
Camping
Grades 1-2, 1-3
Grades 3-4, 4-6

Church School: Youth
Camping

Senior High
Retreats
Junior High
Fellowship groups

Family Life
Celebrations, birthdays
Church activities
Extended family
Family changes
Leisure activities
Work together
Worship

Growth and Relationships
Conflict/hostility
School
Physical growth
Forgiveness/reconciliation
Thankfulness/appreciation
Recreation
Honesty
Independence
Making choices
Cooperation
Sharing
Prejudice
Helping others
Values/attitudes
Responsibility
Loving one another

Music and Rhythmic Activities
Choral readings
Song, hymn, charts
Interpretive movement

Nature: Earth and Universe
Day and night
Mountains
Landscapes
Farms
Rocks and soil
Lakes and rivers

Ecology
Oceans
Moon and stars

Nature: Plant and Animal Life
Animals
Plants
Flowers
Fish
Insects
Birds
Trees

Nature: Seasons and Weather
Spring
Storms
Clouds
Autumn
Snow
Winter
Summer
Wind
Rain

Society
Business
Technology
Discoveries, explorations, research
Industry
Cultural activities
Clothes, food, housing
Transportation
Communications

Stewardship
Alcohol, tobacco, drugs
Care of body and mind
Stewardship of resources
Use of time, abilities
Vacation
Energy conservation
Pollution
Environmental concerns
Conservation of natural resources